D0962297

Wake Up Your Dreams

WAKE UP YOUR DREAMS

A PROVEN STRATEGY TO HELP YOU:

- **Discover** Your Lifelong Dream
- Make **Dream Days** a Regular Part of Your Life
- Avoid **Dream Danger** Zones
- Succeed by Finding a **Dream Partner**

WALT KALLESTAD

ZondervanPublishingHouse
Grand Rapids, Michigan

A Division of HarperCollins*Publishers*

Wake Up Your Dreams
Copyright © 1996 by Walther P. Kallestad

Requests for information should be addressed to:

📖 ZondervanPublishingHouse
Grand Rapids, Michigan 49530

International Trade Paper Edition 0-310-21077-1

Library of Congress Cataloging-in-Publication Data

Kallestad, Walther P., 1948–
    Wake up your dreams : a proven strategy to help you discover your lifelong dream,
make "dream days" a regular part of your life, avoid "dream danger" zones, succeed by
finding a "dream partner" / Walt Kallestad.
        p.   cm.
    Includes bibliographical references (p.   ).
    ISBN: 0–310–20727–4 (hardcover : alk. paper)
    1. Success—Religious aspects—Christianity.   I. Title.
BV4598.3.K35   1996
248.4—dc20   96–8810
                                                                              CIP

This edition printed on acid-free paper and meets the American National Standards Institute Z39.48 standard.

Interior design by Sherri L. Hoffman

Printed in the United States of America

96 97 98 99 00 01 02 /❖ DH/ 10 9 8 7 6 5 4 3 2 1

To my wife and best friend, Mary:
a dream come true

CONTENTS

ACKNOWLEDGMENTS

Special thanks:

To Rose Jackson, a special dream mate, who took my scribbles and scripts and helped me turn them into inspiring dream dynamics

To Ann Spangler, who helped me dig deeper and develop the dream themes, and Stan Gundry, for believing in me and my dreams

To Evelyn Bence for arranging the manuscript with the grace of a world-class composer.

ONE

Nothing Is Impossible For Those Who Dream

I WAS JUST BEGINNING my career as a minister in Phoenix
when I went downtown to hear a world-famous eighty-year-old
gentleman who was winding up his career. Norman Vincent Peale
pulled at his suspenders and, in a calm, assuring way, said something I yearned for the whole world to hear and understand. I had
been applying what he said to my own life, and it was working. To
the crowd of attentive listeners he said,

> To achieve anything significant, everyone needs a little imagi-
> nation and a big dream.

As I sat there, I wondered how many millions felt they were living below their potential. Every day of my life, I encounter people
who struggle with the notion that greater energies, more creative
ideas, and more effective problem-solving abilities are locked up
inside of them. I have dedicated my life to help others unlock that
untapped potential and dream big dreams.

As I use it, the word *dream* does not refer to those pictures that
move through our mind's eye when we sleep. The dreams I speak of
are the distinctive hopes and visions stirring in our imaginations and
calling us forward to the future.

It has been my experience that, when dreams are followed
through with commitment, doors begin to open and encouraging
support flows to the dreamer, resulting in realized dreams. The
process of pursuing a dream is not simple, nor is it shallow. Too often

people pass off dreams as idle musings, when the truth is that dreams are the parents of possibilities. Everything, even the most practical of accomplishments, begins with a dream of what is possible.

In 1978, when I came as minister to Community Church of Joy, I had a dream to build a church that offered something to help everyone—of all ages and backgrounds—solve problems, heal hurts, and grow spiritually. I dreamed of building a place where people could experience new ideas and new worship styles, a place of enthusiasm and fun. Today we touch the lives of not only the twelve thousand Arizonans who participate in our church's activities but also the lives of people around the world. By the year 2000, we expect that roughly fifty thousand ministers and church leaders from all over the globe will have taken part in seminars we regularly offer to help encourage, train, and equip them to meet needs and build dreams.

This all began with one dream.

CAPTURING THE DREAM

DREAMS ARE PLANTED DEEPLY within our hearts and minds. Dreams are part of what God created us to be and to become. When we get a thought or an idea, it may turn into a fulfilled dream, or it may not. Whether it does or doesn't depends on what we do with it. If we take the thought and act on it, we are on the way to discovering the foundational dream beneath the thought.

Capturing the dream is like digging for gold. On the surface, the ground may look like nothing more than a pile of rocks or a weed-infested plot. Deep down, however, lies a treasure waiting to be discovered. To uncover it requires much digging and hard work. That's what capturing the dream is all about—digging to discover the treasure of our dreams. We may have to dig very deep, and we may have to work long and hard before our dream dig pays off.

No great dream is superficial or a mere fantasy. Great dreams require digging beyond surface limitations or past failures or easy-way-out distractions. Dreamers must be actively, passionately digging to bring to light the treasure of their dreams.

A few examples from times past: William Lloyd Garrison, born in 1805 in Massachusetts, grew up believing that slavery was a detestable offense against both God and humanity. He dreamed what must have seemed an impossible dream: *I will one day eliminate slavery in this land.* Garrison dared to dream this in a day when slavery in the United States, in the North as well as the South, was economically profitable and firmly entrenched. The influential governing body of one church declared that slavery was instituted by God. Key national figures insisted that the whole nation depended on slavery.

But Garrison crafted his dream into a hammer that continually pounded against the boulder of slavery. A leading abolitionist, he edited and published *The Liberator*, an abolitionist newspaper, from his home for over thirty years. Advocates of slavery retaliated with sneers and jeers, but Garrison didn't dream alone. Other dreamers, like Frederick Douglass, Sojourner Truth, Levi Coffin, and Harriet Beecher Stowe continued to pound away until all their hammers together became a mighty force that shook the nation with the truth that slavery must be eliminated. Their passion, courage, and commitment made possible a dream that had seemed impossible.

> *Great dreams require digging beyond surface limitations or past failures or easy-way-out distractions.*

Consider Ansel Adams, another dreamer who dug deep. His vision for the preservation of the wild places he photographed was instrumental in encouraging President Franklin D. Roosevelt and Congress to establish a national park in California's Kings Canyon. His own foresight and his awe-inspiring photographs of the grandeur and fragile wonder of the natural world helped secure and preserve wilderness for generations of Americans. Ansel Adams uncovered the treasured dream of a natural heritage of awe and beauty.

Dissuaded by his family from pursuing his dream of working in the theater, Oscar Hammerstein attended Columbia Law School and worked for a year in a law office. But he could not abandon his dream. Unable to shake the certainty that he belonged elsewhere, he finally convinced his uncle to give him a job as an assistant stage manager. From that beginning, Hammerstein went on to write lyrics for numerous stage productions and movies. After composing lyrics for a dozen soon-forgotten musicals, Hammerstein wrote a libretto and lyrics for a production with his new collaborator, Richard Rodgers. *Oklahoma!* ran for five years and 2,212 performances. Hammerstein's legacy of lyrics, in shows such as *South Pacific*, *The King and I*, and *The Sound of Music*, still inspires the world, encouraging people to dig persistently and expectantly "till you find your dream."

Enough from the history books. People are still digging here and now. Tracy Miller is a thirty-two-year-old paraplegic who lost full use of her legs in a 1979 auto accident. In 1988, after years of commitment and plain hard work—pursuing her dream—Tracy won four silver medals in Seoul, South Korea, as a member of the U.S. Paraplegic Racing Team. And on May 13, 1995, Tracy set new women's land speed records for an arm-powered vehicle in both the two-hundred-meter and thousand-meter distances. Tracy's dream, along with the dreams of other disabled athletes, helps push back the limits for all dream-abled people. Tracy's dream is a treasure that encourages all of us to keep on digging.

Think of how the world has been enriched because these people treasured their dreams. What if they hadn't valued their dreams?

TAKE YOUR DREAMS SERIOUSLY

DREAMS ARE SERIOUS BUSINESS. If we take dreams lightly, we miss all their power and potential. Many voices around us suggest that we should embrace pragmatists and realists but discount dreamers. They should be given less stature, we're told, because ideas and imagination are not dependable.

Certainly we all need to work hard and honestly and be realistic. But without new ideas, new thoughts, and imagination, medical research would come to a screeching halt. Technology would come to a standstill. New jobs might never be created. Education would stagnate. Even one single dream that is overlooked, ignored, or discarded could mean the difference between living and dying for multitudes of people.

Dr. Robert S. Flinn and his wife, Irene, invested their lives in their dream of improving the quality of life for the people of Arizona. Dr. Flinn was a heart specialist in more ways than one. As a physician at St. Joseph's Hospital, he paid in advance the bills of patients he knew were indigent. He also volunteered his services several times a week at another hospital in Phoenix's inner city.

Irene Flinn used her financial resources to meet needs wherever she saw them. If she read that a family's home had burned to the ground, she anonymously sent money to help them rebuild. She gave her time to neighborhood and city projects to help others.

The Flinns together supported student nurses, struggling young doctors, community health care projects, arts organizations, and educational opportunities—investing their time and resources wherever they saw a need, to make life better for others.

The Flinns were so committed to their dream that they made provision for their work to continue, through the Flinn Foundation, even after they were gone. Each year, through the Flinn Scholars Program, the Flinn Foundation gives twenty young dreamers—twenty of the top high school seniors in Arizona—a chance to launch their own dreams, giving them full four-year scholarships to any Arizona university, as well as diverse opportunities to travel and learn from others who have realized a dream. Each year, the Flinn Scholars Program graduates Rhodes, Truman, and Fulbright scholars. More important, every year the world is enriched by a new crop of dreamers who believe their lives can, and should, make a difference.

The scope of the Flinns' dream is astounding, but more amazing is the realization that behind the programs and numbers are individual lives and hearts, healed and enriched and changed for good because Robert and Irene Flinn took the seed of one simple dream seriously enough to commit their lives to it.

Your God-inspired dreams are worth investing your life in, worth everything it takes to make them come true. People who have lived out their dreams come to the end of their lives happy and fulfilled. Listen to your dreams. Lean on them. Your life is shaped by your dreams.

Don't Minimize Your Dreams

WHAT IS YOUR TREASURED dream? Have you ever known or even asked yourself? Every dream is important, yet it's so easy to minimize a dream.

You may feel as if your dream is insignificant, that nothing will be changed if you don't pursue it. But every dream has an impact beyond its "size."

I think of an image I saw years ago in an educational film. Picture a room filled with hundreds of set mousetraps. On each mousetrap sits a Ping-Pong ball. One single Ping-Pong ball, no bigger than any of the others, is tossed into the room. Its first bounce launches one ball, and each succeeding bounce sets off another ball. The chain reaction multiplies quickly as each bouncing ball triggers another, until, in a matter of seconds, the room is alive with balls bouncing everywhere.

Does it take a massive amount of energy to *initiate* such a dynamic change? It requires only someone to set one small Ping-Pong ball in motion. The same is true for us. One "small" dream set in motion is powerful enough to unleash the potential in other dreamers and, dream by dream, to reshape the world.

Every dream is important to someone else. In a family, for example, a mother's or father's dream will impact both the children and the spouse. The children's dreams will impact their friends and classmates. Touched by the dream, the spouse will have an impact on work associates and other people in the community. Like ripples spreading from one small pebble tossed in a pond, each dream generates another.

In 1962, Marion Stoddart—wife, mother, homemaker—moved to Groton, Massachusetts, on the banks of the Nashua River. The river derived its name from early Native American people who called it *Nash-a-way*, meaning River With the Pebbled Bottom. But neither Marion nor anyone else could even see the bottom of the Nashua in 1962. The river—fouled and clogged with waste, fibers, and pulp from the many textile and paper mills, cities, and factories lining its banks—didn't run clear but was instead colored by whatever dye had been dumped into it that day.

Looking upon the turbid waters of a dead river, Marion envisioned a river clean and clear again, with trees lining its banks. She envisioned industrialists, business people, homemakers, and citizens coming together to implement a conservation plan for the entire Nashua watershed. The dream caught fire in Marion's life.

> One "small" dream set in motion is powerful enough to unleash the potential in other dreamers and, dream by dream, to reshape the world.

She contacted the state to establish a greenway along the Nashua, but the state of Massachusetts wasn't interested in buying land to plant trees along a dead river. Knowing her dream needed other minds, hands, and voices if it was to become a reality, Marion spoke to people all along the river, sharing her vision and organizing the Nashua River Cleanup Committee.

Through her passion and persistence, Marion inspired others—businessmen and women, teenagers, people of all ages and walks of life—to sign petitions, to speak out at town meetings, to get their hands dirty clearing trash from the Nashua's banks and bottom, and to lobby for changes in a law that would enable cleanup and protection for the Nashua and other rivers. In 1966—after just four years—their citizens' campaign successfully resulted in the passage of the Massachusetts Clean Water Act. The Nashua is now clean enough to be home to bass, pickerel, German brown trout, and perch. Great blue herons, ospreys, and bald eagles once again fish its waters. Today the Nashua runs along forested banks, and pebbles shine up from its bottom through clear water, thanks to the clear vision of Marion Stoddart, "just" a homemaker with a dream.[1]

Don't minimize the effects or reach of your dream. Everyone knows that Teflon gives us nonstick pans, but that same material has lifesaving uses as a critical component in artificial arteries and heart valves as well as in skin patches that help burn victims.

Innovations in pollution control, auto design, and water filtration systems are based on research originally conducted for the space program. Protective outer garments for people who work in hazardous environments, a lightweight breathing apparatus for firefighters, fire-resistant textiles, and even the cushioning system for your favorite athletic shoes all come from NASA research in space suit technology. And there are numerous space research spin-offs in the field of medicine: CAT scanners and digital radiography, X-ray imaging systems, equipment and techniques for speedy separation of biological compounds for diagnostic tests. The list goes on and on.

Don't discount your dreams because you think you are too old; aging shouldn't mean stagnation. Also, don't dismiss your dreams because you think you don't have the proper academic credentials.

I've met some people who've minimized their dreams because they think their dreams aren't "spiritual" enough. They don't aspire to be a Billy Graham. They have no "call" to be a great preacher; therefore, they're sure that their dreams don't count for much in God's grand plan. That simply isn't true. Jesus tells us in the Bible that even a dream as simple as giving a cup of water to someone who is thirsty gives God great pleasure: "I tell you the truth, anyone who gives you a cup of water in my name . . . will certainly not lose his reward."[2]

Perhaps your dreams include feeding hungry people, caring for children, developing an honest business, or serving your community. If it lifts, encourages, teaches, heals, strengthens, and restores people, it should not be discounted or dismissed as being insignificant. In a later chapter, I will address at length how to discern whether a dream is worthy of pursuit: Is it a dream or a scheme? For now I simply challenge you to be open to what God desires to communicate and complete through your dreams.

Don't Dump Your Dreams

WHEN WE ARE UNDER pressure to meet life's deadlines and demands, we often dump our dreams. When fatigue drains us, we can't find the energy to act on our dreams. Negative voices, real or recorded in our memory, distract us from living out our dreams.

When a dreamer stops dreaming, it affects lives and, in ways we may think imperceptible, it affects the world. Louis Pasteur, if you remember, startled the world of science by stating that microorganisms in the air could cause diseases. As a young man, Pasteur placed fifteenth out of twenty-two candidates on his first attempt at the entrance exam for the École Normale in Paris. Had Pasteur given up digging for his dream of a scientific career, the world would have waited much longer for immunization to become a powerful tool in medicine; countless lives would have been lost as a result.

I almost "dumped a dream" that was planted the day I was born. On Sunday morning, September 5, 1948, when the doctor placed me in her arms for the first time, my mother shouted, "I got my minister!" As a young boy I would play "church," setting up rows of chairs in my room, placing a box "pulpit" on my bed, and inviting the family to my church service. I even took up an offering that I brought with me on Sundays to the real church where my father was the minister.

People often asked me—the preacher's son—if I was going to be a minister, and I always answered, "Yup." My aspiration—my dream—may have been obvious. At the end of every Sunday service, I ran to the door and stood proudly by my dad, shaking hands with the worshipers.

But reality dealt my dream a harsh blow when I was ten years old. One evening I heard loud voices shouting in the living room. Slipping out of bed, I slid down the stairs and lay outside the door, listening as angry men told my dad to get out of town. Tears began to roll down my face as I heard the arguments. Crawling back up the wooden staircase, I threw myself on my bed and cried myself to sleep. Was that what my dream had in store for me?

Growing up in a minister's home, I learned how much pain ministers often endure. I began to think maybe I wasn't cut out for this. As the years passed, I decided a better dream might be to become a businessman and get on a church board to support the minister. I would be the best possible friend and advocate.

In college, I majored in sociology and became a community youth worker. When I was twenty-seven, deep from within my heart the dream to go to seminary and become an ordained minister reemerged. I talked it over with Dr. Rogness, a former president of Luther Theological Seminary, who gave me some curious advice: If I could possibly stay away, I should. But if I found I just couldn't stay away, I should come, because that meant God was calling me to be a minister. I now see the wisdom of his advice. I expect he wanted me to be sure the dream was mine—and from God—and not simply my mother's dream for me.

The support of my wife, Mary, gave me another major confirmation that I should pursue the dream. If I were to go to seminary, it would mean enormous sacrifices for Mary and me and our two children. We would have to sell our home. Both Mary and I would have to work extra hours to earn enough to support our young family. In spite of those sacrifices, Mary shared the dream with me. Her support and encouragement provided the steam I needed to stay with a dream that I feel God placed deep within my spirit.

Claim Your Dreams

ONE NIGHT, RITA LEARNED what a treasure dreams are when she awoke coughing from the smoke of fire consuming her home. Quickly she ran into her son's room to rescue him. On her way out, she was able to grab the only other living creature in her household. Clinging to her little boy and her cat, she stood outside, watching everything she owned turn to ashes.

When the fire was finally extinguished, she walked through the charred embers and cried out, "I still have my dreams! Nothing can destroy my dreams." The fire had consumed her house, her car, her jewelry, her furniture, her clothes, and her artwork, but Rita still had her dreams. Though fires, earthquakes, hurricanes, and other destructive forces can wipe out possessions, they cannot touch a dream. Think about it: How often do we value perishable possessions more highly than we do our dreams? We work so hard to amass more "stuff." Imagine what dreams could come true if we harnessed the same energy to dig out and live out our dreams!

Live Your Dream

DOROTHEA JACKSON WAS IN her early sixties when she set in motion a lifelong dream to be a teacher. She started by volunteering as a docent naturalist "interpreter" at the Arizona-Sonora Desert Museum in Tucson. That meant weeks and months of serious studies in botany, zoology, geology, and biology. But those studies, coupled with more than ten thousand hours spent answering questions of visitors on the museum grounds and taking nature programs to children in local schools, prompted her to drive her camper cross-country to attend national zoological conferences, to hike in volcanic fields in Mexico, to raft the Colorado River, to explore caves, and to staff displays at local malls on environmental issues.

At sixty-eight, Dorothea went back to college to study botany, specifically lichenology, earning a bachelor's degree from Arizona State University at age seventy-one. She says she never had any trouble keeping up with—or feeling out of place with—the considerably younger people in her classes. Despite some concessions to age, like stopping for frequent breaks when she walks, not going places with elevations above five thousand feet, and sometimes staying in motels rather than camping when she's on the road, Dorothea's mental vigor and vitality belie her eighty-two years. This is due in no small part to her attitude. She encourages people of all ages to get up and do, saying, "If you can't think of something to do, you can always think of something to learn."

People who keep dreaming keep growing. Without dreams we may *exist* seventy or eighty years, but we will not fully participate in the grand adventure that life can be. Do you want to live your life? Live your dreams.

DARE TO DREAM

OVER LUNCH, JERRY COLANGELO, the owner of the Phoenix Suns, recently told me how he arrived in Phoenix in March 1968, with his wife, three children, eight suitcases, and a dream. As a kid, he listened to Cubs games on the radio and dreamed of what a ballpark must look like. Today he is building a ballpark with a retractable roof that will open to reveal a canopy of stars. Jerry's dream of owning a championship basketball team and a big-league baseball team, the Arizona Diamondbacks, has come true. It's important, says Jerry, to take your dreams seriously—because dreams are the forerunners of fact.

Every dream is the parent of possibilities—and the parent of problems as well. I understand both firsthand. That is why I have poured so much passion into this book and why I want it to help you with your dreams.

I first thought about writing a book about living our dreams eight years ago. I talked to a publisher who seemed interested, but he retired a few months later. My dream to write the book, however, kept growing within me. I saw the possibilities and set out to solve the problems.

I appreciated the encouragement that people gave me along the way. One person suggested I write a book on prayer; another thought I should write a book on leadership. I ended up writing books on both subjects. In fact, I've written five other books before getting to this book. The journey brought learning, adventure, and challenge, but, over the past eight years, I never lost sight of writing this book on dreaming.

This book is a reality because I dared to dream. If we can remember that dreams—and even the problems that come with them—are parents of possibilities, those dreams can help us see the invisible, believe the incredible, and achieve the impossible.

In these pages, I want to lay out practical ways to help you recognize your dreams, learn from mistakes, and avoid the pitfalls that surround every dream. I am convinced that no one can live— truly live—without a dream. My earnest prayer is that this book will give you the confidence that nothing is impossible for those who dare to dream.

As I worked through various drafts of this book, my wife, Mary, suggested that perhaps the most significant contribution I could make would be to help each reader discover a dream for his or her own life. The next few chapters deal extensively with the issue of identifying and clarifying your dream. But even before we get to the chapter on finding your focus, you might ask yourself some preliminary questions: What excites you? What beckons you to a bright future? What gives you hope?

> **Dreams can help us see the invisible, believe the incredible, and achieve the impossible.**

What is your dream? Do you know? The answers to the following questions may help you find a dream. On a separate sheet of paper, try to answer each question in as much detail as possible.

1. What do you most enjoy doing?
2. What do you do best?
3. When you daydream, what do you think about most?
4. What do you want to learn more about?
5. If you had a day to do absolutely anything you wanted, what would you do?
6. What touches your emotions more than anything else?
7. What have you received the most compliments for doing?
8. What captures your interest most?

9. Whom do you most admire, and why?
10. What are the basic characteristics of, or skills involved in, the occupations you most respect?
11. What are you most confident about?
12. What would you be willing to exchange your life for?

Your answers to these twelve questions can help you begin to find a direction for a dream. Go ahead and dare to dream. And know that the choice is yours: Forge ahead or forget about it. If you choose to forge ahead, my hope is that this book can help you live your dreams beyond whatever limits you think you have today. Ask God to help you wake up the dreams buried deep in your heart and soul.

TWO

ঔℐℛ

Twenty-Twenty
Dreaming

WHAT I CALL _twenty-twenty dreaming_ helped sustain James Nesmith during seven horrendous years as a prisoner of war in North Vietnam. Major Nesmith had virtually no contact or communication with anyone, no room to move and no physical activity, no occupation for his mind. If he was going to maintain his sanity, he knew he had to find some way to engage his mind.

A weekend golfer with an average in the midnineties before his capture, Major Nesmith set his mind to improving his game. Down to the most minute detail, he visualized every hole of his favorite golf course. Each day, he envisioned his stance, his swing, his follow-through—every element of his game, every aspect of the course.

After seven years of focused twenty-twenty dreaming, Nesmith was released, free to come home. As you can imagine, he was eager to pick up his golf clubs and test his skill. Now, get this: His first time back on a course, Nesmith shot an incredible seventy-four, a testimony to the astounding power of a clearly focused dream.[1]

Consider the world of eyes and optics. Let's start with the obvious. To function at life's optimum, we need a clear, sharply focused image of our surroundings. Twenty-twenty vision requires a careful collaboration of the components of the eye: the cornea, iris, lens, ciliary muscles, retina, optic nerve, and the length of the eyeball itself. In nearsightedness, the focused image of anything more than twenty feet away falls in front of the retina. That means the nearsighted person sees a fuzzy, blurry, indistinct image of anything "out ahead."

Now return with me to the world of people who dare to dream. When it comes to setting one's sights on the future, it's important to see a clear, sharply focused image of your dream. That's the key to capturing the dream and making it a functional reality.

Many people aspire to do something significant in their lifetime. They want to live for a noble purpose, but they haven't a clue as to what that purpose might be. Others may have an idea, but a fuzzy one. What I call twenty-twenty dreaming will help you recognize and realize your dreams. The more clearly focused and detailed your dream is, the more likely it will come true.

> Seeing a clear, sharply focused image of your dream is the key to capturing the dream and making it a functional reality.

Most dreams fail because of fuzzy focus. If you've been in a movie theater, you know the audience can't long endure the discomfort of a fuzzy screen before someone shouts, "Focus!"

And who doesn't know the disappointment of opening a packet of eagerly anticipated photographs, just back from the processor, only to find that a cherished memento is an unrecognizable blur. Fuzzy focus in our dreams leaves us feeling disturbed and discouraged. Ultimately our dreams will be unfulfilled.

In optometry and photography, one can make adjustments that improve focus. It takes the right lens, the right light; in photography, it also takes the right distance from the subject.

Similarly, sharpening your dream focus involves identifying the "subject," determining how "far away" it is (how long will you need and what resources?), and recognizing how much "available light"—understanding, ability, sound advice, God's guidance—you have.

The incredible resolution obtainable in today's high-altitude photography is due primarily to new defect-free lenses that are ground to extremely precise tolerances, and to highly sensitive films. The fine focus available with these lenses means sharp images, even of small objects, from distances of forty thousand feet and more.

Clarifying a dream takes hard work and single-minded focus. How we align our focus is key to determining the results of our dreams. With laser light, unlike ordinary diffused light, the troughs and crests that form each light wave align with the troughs and crests of the other light waves around it. This makes the light coherent—one straight, powerful, focused beam. As dreamers we need to align our intent, our thoughts, and our actions with God's to aim them unswervingly, powerfully, clearly toward our dreams.

As you think in terms of sharpening your dream's focus—your dream's purpose—you'll want to ask some basic questions:

Where is my dream going?
Why is my dream important?
What is most important about my dream?
Who will my dream benefit most?
How is my dream going to come true?
When will my dream be successful?

In this chapter, I'll focus in on the first of these questions. A key question is front and center: Where is my dream going?

BEGIN WITH THE END IN MIND

EVERY GREAT DREAM BEGINS with the end in mind. I challenge you to live "as if" the dream has already come true.

The more actualized the dream is in the beginning, the stronger the dream grows. By beginning with the end, you can foresee potential problems and obstacles, and conceive and work toward solutions that prevent problems. Keeping the end in mind strengthens us to endure and surmount obstacles when they arise. Backing up, from the dreaming to the doing, increases the chances for the dream's success.

Mike Hollman's life has been filled with suffering and setbacks, but Mike has dreamed his way back to health and happiness, even after medical doctors had given up on him.

Ten years ago, Mike was involved in a serious automobile accident that left him facing eight eye surgeries, memory loss, a kidney transplant, removal of half a lung and two toes, ripped muscles, shattered bones, diabetes and circulation problems, and numerous daily vomiting episodes. Any one of these obstacles would be enough to derail a human spirit.

Before the accident, Mike was a professional golfer. Today he dreams and pushes ahead with the end in mind of a full recovery. Even though he remains in pain about 80 percent of the time, Mike loves to teach and play golf. Not long ago, because of his limited vision, Mike lost a dozen golf balls on the first four holes. That didn't dissuade him; he continues to use every ounce of his energy to dig out, and live out, his dream. What keeps Mike moving forward?

Mike says it's his dream. He stays focused and knows where he is going.

Is the "end" simply too vague in your mind for you to envision? If so, let me comment on the practical exercise found in Keith Miller's book *Ten Minute Magic*. To help clarify dreams, Keith suggests compiling a personal "dream book" in which a dreamer places pictures or images from magazines, newspapers, or picture books to represent one's dreams. Beautiful pictures of real estate developments or places you want to visit, a picture of a family that enjoys spending time together or of someone working with the homeless and poor—these images can represent a goal. Pictures provide stimulation for dreaming.

For example, Keith wrote about one woman whose first dream was personal freedom. She cut out a picture of a painting of a magnificent American bald eagle soaring through the sky. It was a powerful image.

Keith also suggests gluing such pictures representing dreams on three-by-five cards so you can carry them in a purse or car or organizer. By taking a few minutes every day to look through a "dream book," your mind will be motivated and your spirit inspired to seize and secure your dream.[2]

Pictures are often much more powerful than written words. That is why our individual dream picture books can prove to be a practical help at every stage of clarifying and living out our dreams. Daily we are bombarded verbally from our society, which relies heavily on left-brain thinking-reasoning and rationalization. When we introduce new thoughts and ideas through pictures, we activate the right side of our brains, working in the realm of the visual and sensory. As we do so, we can become more open to possibilities. Thinking through pictures can greatly enhance the sharp focus and successful realization of our dreams.

DREAMS OR SCHEMES?

YOU MAY BE ABLE to see an "end" you want to reach, but before you start going for that goal, stop and ask yourself some very serious questions that are at the heart of this book and my philosophy: Why is my dream important? Whom will my dream benefit?

Yes, I'm a dreamer. Yes, everyone can—and should—dream and live great dreams. But not every dream deserves pursuing. Some great dreams are simply schemes. What do I mean?

Schemes are selfish, primarily benefiting oneself. Schemes result in self-aggrandizement. Schemers grow greedy to line their own pockets. They want the accolades. They place their needs ahead of the needs of anyone else. To schemers, ethics, morals, and values are relative. They use people and abuse power.

> Great dreamers possess servants' hearts. Dreamers are givers, not takers.

Great dreamers, on the other hand, possess servants' hearts. A schemer asks, "What can I get?" A dreamer asks, "What can I give?"

Dreamers are givers, not takers. Energizing and enthusiastic, they empower and encourage others to go beyond themselves and dream big dreams. They live by the highest standards of ethics, morality, and values. Dreamers build the world; schemers erode it.

Great Dreams Build the World

AS HUMANS CREATED IN the image of God, we were created to dream. God designed into us the capacity to dream. You and I are more than a mass of molecules, more than just another species. Dreams are part of what makes us more than that. We are made in the image of the Creator of dreams—the ultimate Dream Maker.

The biblical story of creation is fascinating. The Genesis account begins with God's grand dream. He created the heavens and the earth, and then light. He created fertile land separated by waters, and then vegetation, birds, and animals. God saw that everything created was good, but this excellent creation needed excellent management. That's when God created men and women "in his own image."

You and I were created to be trustees of God's dreams: "God blessed them and said to them [men and women], 'Be fruitful and increase in number; fill the earth and subdue it. Rule over the fish of the sea and the birds of the air and over every living creature that moves on the ground.'"[3] Animals and birds are not creative dreamers and doers; men and women are. Humankind is the custodian of the resources of the planet—minerals, trees, land, water, air, and everything else God provided to sustain life and to enhance living in the fullest sense.

The ability to dream is a God-given legacy. What an incredible opportunity has been given to us to be partners in creation, to dream, to contribute, to accomplish amazing things!

We have a responsibility to find ways to keep our world mentally, emotionally, physically, and spiritually fresh without compromising biblical principles and truth. God would not lay that responsibility upon us without giving us the means to do it through the resources of his ability.

Millard Fuller was a millionaire by the time he was thirty. At this point in his life, his business consumed him to the point that he succeeded financially, but failed relationally. One day, he came home to find an empty house. His wife, Linda, and the children had left him. That unnerving shock led Millard to take stock of his life and to reconsider his priorities.

Millard reassessed his life's dream, and he and Linda were able to restore their relationship. In fact, Millard and Linda began to build a new dream together: a dream that every person on earth could have a decent home. That was forty thousand homes ago. The dream has become Habitat for Humanity, a nonprofit organization through which volunteers work alongside needy people hoping to own their own homes, to erect or refurbish affordable housing that will be made available at cost. The potential owners must contribute two hundred hours of work, either on their own home or on other Habitat projects, and must meet their mortgage payments, which are interest free. In 1993, Habitat for Humanity built an average of 23 homes a day in over 900 cities in 40 countries.[4]

Millard and Linda Fuller's dream has captured the imagination of ordinary people—lawyers, teachers, builders, weekend do-it-yourselfers, homemakers, business people—and people like Jimmy and Rosalynn Carter and Paul Newman, who all work side by side to build homes and dreams. That's the kind of great dream that builds up—rather than destroys—community and God's created world.

Great Dreams Travel Two-Way Streets

BEFORE WE TALK OF great win-win dreams, let me tell you of one memorable losing scheme. One day a well-mannered gentleman walked into our church office. He claimed to be a medical doctor. He needed help, he said, because his car, wallet, and clothing had been stolen. My assistant minister listened to his convincing story and invited the man to stay in his home with him and his family until everything could be worked out.

Every day, this man would leave to go to work in a local hospital. His amazing communication skills and vocabulary convinced the powers that be to let him scrub up and join medical teams in surgical suites.

Claiming to be an heir to a major beer producer in Germany, he assured everyone that thousands of dollars were being wired to him within two weeks. But in the midst of his elaborate con, little inconsistencies began to show up. Enough doubt arose that my father and I quietly went to a police friend to help us check out this guy.

An investigation proceeded, and late one night federal agents arrested one of the most-wanted international white-collar criminals in Europe. I was amazed at the way this man schemed his way through life. Everything he planned was only for his advantage; it didn't matter who lost, so long as he won.

All schemes, large and small, have one objective: "You must lose so that I can win." Quite the opposite is true for dreaming. The objective of a dream should be "win-win." It's frequently true, in fact, that many of our own dreams come true while we are helping other people achieve their dreams.

At a recent seminar in Phoenix, Zig Ziglar said that we can get everything we could possibly need in life if we are willing to help enough people get what they need. As our staff at Community Church of Joy works with our city's planning and zoning commission, the commission asks a good question: How will our dream benefit the community? You see, sound dreams always travel two-way streets.

Great Dreams Call Us to Grow

DREAMS STRETCH AND STIMULATE us to become all God created us to be. The writer of Psalm 139 painted a beautiful portrait of the creation of a human being: "For you created my inmost being; you knit me together in my mother's womb. I praise you because I am . . . wonderfully made; your works are wonderful, I know that full well."[5]

God created each of us wonderfully for a wonderful purpose: "For we are God's workmanship, created in Christ Jesus to do good works, which God prepared in advance for us to do."[6] God has planted a great dream in each of us that will call us to excellence and maturity.

Great dreams will call us forward to stretch and learn and grow. Dr. Albert Bandura of Stanford University notes, "I believe we are not content with what we already know and can do; we want action and growth—opportunities to explore our competence and mastery. Young or old, we want to be challenged." Psychologists studying aging have found that "growth and mastery" are keys to a sense of well-being in older adults. Succeeding in new endeavors raises what Dr. Bandura calls our *self-efficacy*, our belief in our capacity to achieve, which in turn, it appears, influences us to pursue and stick with healthy and mentally stimulating activities.[7]

> *Because of the dynamic nature of life, we either grow or decline. The gift of our dreams calls us to grow.*

Every great dream keeps us growing. Life is not static. Because of the dynamic nature of life, we either grow or decline. The gift of our dreams calls us to grow.

Great Dreams and Great Dreamers Rely on God

IF OUR DREAMS RELY on God, then God needs to be trustworthy. How reliable is God? A look at the life of Jesus reveals that God kept every promise he ever made about the long-expected Messiah, from his lineage (Genesis 49:10 and Luke 3:33) to the manner of his birth (Isaiah 7:14 and Matthew 1:18); from the place where he was born (Micah 5:2 and Matthew 2:1) to the place his family fled for safety (Hosea 11:1 and Matthew 2:14); from his actions (Isaiah 9:1–2 and Matthew 4:12–16) and attributes (Isaiah 11:2 and Luke 2:52) to the reactions of others to him (Isaiah 53:3 and John 1:11); from his betrayal by a friend (Psalm 41:9 and Mark 14:10) to the actions of his executioners (Psalm 22:18 and Mark 15:24); from the manner of his death (Isaiah 53:12 and Matthew 27:38) to his victorious resurrection (Psalm 16:10 and Matthew 28:9). What God said he would do, he did. The saying goes, "Nobody bats a thousand," but God does.

God is reliable because God is the ultimate authority. He is our creator, and he knows how life works best. We can trust God to reliably guide our dreams. As president, Abraham Lincoln was the man in authority, the man the nation looked to for leadership and sound judgment at a time when the union itself was imperiled. Lincoln said, "I know that the Lord is always on the side of right. But it is my constant anxiety and prayer that I and this nation should be on the Lord's side."[8] With the dreams of the country at stake, Lincoln turned to the Bible and to God in prayer because he believed God was the ultimate authority and would reliably guide him to make the wisest decisions possible.

> Our dreams realize their greatest potential when they are built on a consistent foundation. God is that and more.

God is reliable because he has integrity. God's character is flawless; his word is his honor. When King David sang a song of thanks to God for delivering David from his enemies, he asserted, "As for God, his way is perfect; the word of the Lord is flawless."[9]

God is reliable because he is constant. Everything around us may change, but the Bible says, "Jesus Christ is the same yesterday, today, and forever."[10] Our dreams realize their greatest potential when they are built on a consistent foundation. God is that and more.

Finally, God is reliable because he cares for and loves you and me. William Manchester attributes the fierce loyalty that Douglas MacArthur elicited from his troops to several factors: he was nearer the age of his men than were the other senior officers, and, most notably, he shared the discomfort they endured and the danger they faced and cared for his men deeply. "The word is *love*. Nothing . . .

absolutely nothing pulls a team closer together or strengthens the lines of loyalty more than love.... It promotes feelings that say, 'I belong' and ... 'You can trust me because I trust you.'"[11] Because God loves you and me more than anyone else does, we can trust God with our dreams.

FOCUS ON SIGNIFICANCE

AS YOU FOCUS YOUR dream, remember that *significant* dreams are more important than *successful* dreams. If our goal is to become the person God imagined when he first thought of us, that is significant. If our dream improves life's quality, that is significant. If our dream is realized as we *become* people of character and excellence, not just as we track what we *do*, that is significant.

I'm inspired by this account, written by Russell O'Quinn, who was named one of the top five test pilots in the United States by *Life* magazine in 1984. He is president of Aerospace Design and Development Company, the country's first civilian high-performance flight test company. O'Quinn thanks God for bringing him to a point where his lifelong dream came true.

He describes his thoughts one morning several years ago. He'd been chosen to test a new weapons system to be used in Operation Desert Storm—a "fire breather," he called it. "I had about ten minutes to get to the test range, so I had a little time for reflection," O'Quinn writes. "Suddenly it hit me like a ton of bricks. Right now I was living every dream I'd had as a boy. Clark Gable never flew an airplane like this!"

Once in the plane,

> ... reality set in. When Clark Gable did this, he had the strains of the New York Philharmonic playing in the background. I had sweat running out of my helmet clear down to my boot tops. That strange noise in the number two engine that we'd been trying to find for weeks was still there. I wasn't looking forward to performing some of the "top gun" maneuvers that were

printed out on the test cards on my kneeboard. And suddenly I realized that when dreams come true, they aren't always what we expect. . . . Have you ever noticed that a dream come true usually becomes a memory almost instantly? You and I spend an awful lot of time pursuing dreams. If those dreams are not centered in the things that God would have for you, or if you're looking for some utopia in this world, take it from one who has some experience. Whether those dreams come true or not, you're due to be terribly, bitterly disappointed.[12]

Russell O'Quinn found that lasting satisfaction comes from centering our dreams in God. We can succeed with our dreams but find the contentment and rewards that come with success are merely fleeting memories. A dream that is significant, however, holds lasting reward and satisfaction for the dreamer. The key is to look beyond successful completion to the transforming power of significance we find when we center our dreams in God.

A DREAM IN FOCUS

LET ME GIVE YOU an example of a dream—not a scheme—that has been carefully thought out. On a Thursday afternoon not long ago, Ken and George walked into my office eager to present a "dream proposal." It was evident to me that they had gone through the early stage of focusing their purpose.

They're working on some creative computer hardware they hope will eventually revolutionize the worldwide computer industry. Their enthusiasm was contagious. They began their presentation to me at the end of their dream. Their dreaming process started with the end in mind. With a clear picture of the product, they worked backward until they covered every detail of how to best build their dream.

Ken and George held in their hands a hand-built prototype of their product. They presented all their plans for production, marketing, and sales as well. Then came the bottom line. With tears in their eyes, they said that they wanted a significant portion of their profits to go to building our church's new two-hundred-acre campus.

The excitement of knowing what a difference their dream could make in the lives of children, teens, single parents, marriages, families, and the character development of leaders made their dream even sweeter.

Deep in my heart, I was exploding with joy. Imagine the power dreams have as they connect with one another. Before Ken and George left, we prayed that God would help all of us continue to dream and to believe that "all things are possible with God."[13]

EXPERIENCE YOUR DREAM THROUGH GOD'S EYES

NO DREAM INSPIRED BY God is inconsequential. Changing attitudes, relationships, situations, or lives is a big job. God-inspired dreamers want their dreams to make meaningful contributions to the world. They look for ways they can make a positive difference.

A teddy bear seems like an insignificant thing, hardly the stuff of which God-inspired dreams are made. But several years ago God inspired someone—whose name I don't even know—to care about traumatized children caught in the crisis of accidents, child abuse, or separation from their parents. That dreamer envisioned the Teddy Bear Patrol: putting a teddy bear in every police car for the purpose of giving those children a small shred of security, comfort, and hope to cling to in the midst of hurt.

Through other caring hearts this project has come to Phoenix, where the goal is to put five thousand new teddy bears in patrol cars. A local radio station, a communications company, a bank, a local mall, and many children and adults, as well as the Phoenix Police Department, have responded to the tender simplicity of this dream. Simple, yes, but how many children, looking back, will one day thank God for someone who cared enough to envision the difference a small act of love could make in one young heart? Sculpting a better world, heart by heart, requires the best dreams of everyone.

To dream through God's eyes, I commend to you a simple, concise dream discovery process I found in the gospel of Matthew. Jesus is quoting from the Hebrew scriptures:

"'Love the Lord your God with all your heart and with all your soul and with all your mind.' This is the first and greatest commandment. And the second is like it: 'Love your neighbor as yourself.' All the Law and the Prophets hang on these two commandments."[14]

Loving God and loving people is the foundation for everything God desires for us to dream and do. This is the foundation of a dream that God sees as significant.

FOCUSING: A LIFELONG PROCESS

IN THIS CHAPTER, I'VE talked about focusing one's dream. It's a "must" place to start, but don't get the idea that you set your sights on the finish line and then allow yourself to lose sight of the panoramic view.

State Route 89A in Arizona is a highway of majestic beauty. It winds for twelve miles through the narrow gorge and spectacular russet- and buff-colored walls of Oak Creek Canyon. If you are a passenger, the twelve miles are an ever-changing panorama of wonder. But if you are a driver, unless you stop your car at the overlook at the head of the canyon, you will never even be aware of, much less appreciate, the awesome beauty around you. As a driver, all you can afford to appreciate is the immediate tight right turn and the roadway dropping ahead of you in one tortuous switchback after another. To be mindful of anything but the road and traffic ahead is to invite disaster.

The only way to recognize the full panoramic truth of what you're driving through is to take advantage of the occasional pull-off to stop, get out, breathe deeply, and look around you. It's better yet if you take time to scramble down a bank, cross the icy creek, and hike up the trails that wander into side pockets of the canyon. Apart from intentionally taking time to stop and drink it in, there is no way to fully appreciate the power and wonder surrounding you, waiting to be discovered, in Oak Creek Canyon.

Most of us go through life as a driver rather than as a passenger, our eyes grimly focused on the demands of the road immediately ahead of us. I think of an old adage: Work is never done. I am told that, on average, people have thirty-six hours of incomplete work just sitting on top of their desks. When I recognized the implication of that, I decided to respond positively: I created a dream day every Friday to schedule time to dream.

I begin my dream day by tuning in to God through prayer and meditation. After time spent reading my dream "playbook"—the Bible—and listening to hear God's dreams and desires, I journal my thoughts. I record as many details as I can about the dreams capturing my mind, emotions, and spirit. Some dream days I have only an hour; other days I set aside four or more hours. Occasionally I take the entire day to just dream.

During some of my dream times, I write out weekly, monthly, yearly, or long-term goals. At other times I have written and revised personal and professional mission statements. Occasionally I visit places that inspire my imagination, maybe a child-care center or a park, where I talk to people and ask a lot of questions. There are times I go for a walk and let my mind wander and wonder. On some dream days, I may read a book as a dream developer.

> The only waste of time is to live a lifetime and never take the time to dream—to focus it, to plan for it, to live it.

You may think you simply don't have time for a dream day— even a dream hour. But let me assure you that dreaming never wastes time. The only waste of time is to live a lifetime and never take the time to dream—to focus it, to plan for it, to live it.

But I do suggest you find yourself a partner. I recently watched a bowling coach working with a young bowler whose balls consistently veered off into the gutter. After showing the little boy how to keep his feet pointing straight ahead, the coach told him to keep his eyes on the arrows on the lane ahead, not on his feet. The little boy saw immediate results: His aim improved, and his bowling ball rolled down the center of the lane, right on target.

In living out your dream, your walk can be straighter and your aim truer when you have another who believes in you and your dream. It's helpful to find someone to be your coach, your friend, your "dream mate." Just as there are qualities an aspiring athlete should look for in choosing a coach, there are valuable considerations to keep in mind as you look for a "dream mate" to help you realize your dream.

THREE

Everybody Needs
a Dream Mate

ONNIEJO BROWN WAS AN elementary school music
teacher in need of a new dream focus. After years of teaching,
she went back to college—with no declared major and no
idea what she wanted to do. She was clear on only one point: She
wanted "anything but teaching." College counselors at the time didn't
see many options for her and sent her on a math and science route.

So Connie signed up for a human physiology class, unaware that
she was taking a class from a teacher other students dreaded, and
unaware that the chemistry class she was just beginning was a *pre-
requisite* for the physiology course.

There were about twenty students in the class, and Connie
admits that she "couldn't even understand what they were talking
about when they told the teacher what their major was." The professor was incredulous when he asked her why she was taking the
course, and she answered, "For fun." Connie struggled to understand the subject all the way to the bitter end, and she was one of
only five students to complete the course.

This professor, the one with an intimidating reputation, saw in
Connie qualities that Connie didn't even see in herself. The professor
stuck by her. The next semester, and for the next two years, Connie
taught the lab section for the same professor. The professor also suggested to Connie that she should look into medical schools. This
time Connie was incredulous.

But as other professors echoed the same advice, Connie took an aptitude test, which showed she was suited to being a medical doctor. Connie eventually decided that the Lord was nudging her through her professor: Open your eyes. Go for it.

Today Dr. Conniejo Brown, emergency medical specialist, looks back with gratitude to those who saw unrealized potential in her and encouraged her to reach for the best.

To Connie, that professor—and other mentors—were dream mates: people who encouraged her, helped her identify and then live out her dream. A dream mate can point out strengths and abilities that the dreamer may be totally unaware of. A dream mate can help a dreamer say yes to possibilities.

Connie did not actively seek out a dream mate, but I encourage you to do so, at any and every stage of your journey. Every dreamer needs a dream mate—to help focus the dream and then to help live out and achieve the dream. What do I mean by a dream mate? I propose the following profile or "job description." A dream mate:

D   Dares to focus on your significance, not simply your success.
R   Responds to your ideas with respect.
E   Expects the best.
A   Affirms your talents and abilities.
M   Maximizes learning and growth opportunities to improve the dream.

M   Makes the most of mistakes and failures.
A   Accepts only excellence.
T   Takes time to give honest feedback.
E   Encourages you unconditionally and nonjudgmentally to help you persevere.

For a dreamer, a dream mate is not a luxury. The support of a dream mate nourishes, encourages, and sustains a healthy dream and dreamer. People who don't have a dream mate or network of dream mates face almost insurmountable challenges as they try to live out their dreams.

Pat Riley coached the Los Angeles Lakers to a 1980 NBA world championship. In his book *The Winner Within*, Pat shares the story of how, one year later, the Lakers—world champions—were defeated by what he calls "the Disease of Me," an "overpowering belief in their own importance. Their actions virtually shout the claim, 'I'm the one.'"[1] That is a delusion; it is almost impossible to "truly act alone and succeed." The Disease of Me was already at work in the team when the Lakers reassembled for the first day of training camp for the 1980–81 season.

> The support of a dream mate nourishes, encourages, and sustains a healthy dream and dreamer.

Only twice before in NBA history had a defending champion team gone down to defeat the next year in the first playoff round. It happened in 1949 to the Bullets and in 1957 to the Warriors. Because the Disease of Me infected the Laker team, "Greed cruised to the surface—attacking the disciplines, the collaboration, and the flow that enabled us to succeed in the first place."[2] The Lakers executed one of the fastest falls from grace in NBA history. They learned quickly that solo success is not possible; it takes teamwork to succeed at every endeavor.

That applies to dreamers as well as basketball teams. To keep from contracting the Disease of Me, we all need to be part of a "dream team." It is too easy to succumb to that disease and fail without solid dream mates.

One of the key stumbling blocks to professional success, according to leadership consultant Robert Staub, is lack of intimacy; business leaders need to be in relationships that provide feedback so they can see themselves as others see them and understand where others are coming from.[3] Dreamers, as well as business leaders, need the input and support of others to help them get, and stay, on track.

I encourage you to consider the profile of a dream mate and look for people in your life who best fit that description. The right dream mate can help you identify, achieve, and even surpass your life's dream.

It would seem natural to look for a dream mate "close to home," in the form of a supportive family member, a dear friend, a good neighbor—someone you may spend a lot of time with. You may find your number-one dream mate there, but, then again, you may not.

At first blush you'd think the people who know you best would be the best supporters of a new idea, cutting-edge innovation, or breakthrough dream. But the old adage "familiarity breeds contempt" is often true when it comes to building dreams. Sometimes those who are closest to us see only what "is" and are blind to what "can be." Their care and concern for us may lead them to advise us to do the sure thing, not the risky or galvanizing thing.

A friend whose adult son took up scuba diving didn't rejoice to hear that he intended to take his open-water practical training in waters known to be home to hammerhead sharks. Her advice would have been, "Stick to diving in the swimming pool!" But this mother realized that, to reach his goal of scuba certification, her son needed to seek advice from someone with a more objective view and diving experience.

"I've encouraged my son and supported him in so many of the goals and dreams he's had as he was growing up," she says, "but I realized in his first year away at college that his dreams are ranging further; he needs the help of other people, with their knowledge and experience, to help him reach those dreams." This young man needed different dream mates to stand with him for different dreams. And his mother wasn't the perfect match for some of those daring dreams.

Don't assume that your spouse, parent, child, co-worker, or best friend will be the person who helps you reach beyond the status quo. Certainly these are great candidates, but don't put undue pressure on them to take on this role. Some form of change or risk is inherent in any dream, and the people closest to us are the ones with the most at stake, the most to risk, when we pursue those dreams.

Dr. Sidney B. Simon affirms that a change for one person—such as relocating to begin a new job—has a domino effect in the lives of others. "Your success or a step toward it will subtly or dramatically change your relationships with the people around you. They must adjust, and you, in turn, must adapt to their adjustment."[4] A dream's success or failure brings changes to the lives of others. Your dream may have a 90 percent chance of success and only a 10 percent chance of failure, but that 10 percent looms large in the minds of those it would affect directly. Successfully realizing a dream brings changes, too.

You need to take into account the effect your dream will have on the lives of those close to you and approach change cooperatively, but you may need to look outside the circle of your family, friends, or coworkers for a dream mate.

> CAUTION: Not every "life" mate is a dream mate.
> Not every "play" mate is a dream mate.
> Not every "work" mate is a dream mate.
> Not every "soul" mate is a dream mate.

Your dream mate may not be your best friend. What's more, your mate for one dream may not be your mate on other dreams. A dream mate may support you for a season and then, for any number of reasons, withdraw enthusiasm and support.

When looking for members of a "dream team," think in terms of people who will "be there" for you as you dream. Let's turn again to the points of the dream mate profile.

DARES TO FOCUS ON YOUR SIGNIFICANCE, NOT SIMPLY YOUR SUCCESS

A DREAM MATE SHOULD dare to join you in dreaming dreams of significance. Everyone wants to become successful in life endeavors. That's great, but that's incomplete. Success impacts life, but it does not necessarily *improve* life; significance does. Significance impels people to move, and to live, far beyond where they are today. Great dream mates help dreamers become more than successful; they help them to become *significant*.

My wife, Mary, is a great example of a dream mate dedicated to helping me dream significant dreams. When I first began preaching to a congregation, I would ask Mary, "How was the message today?" Mary always evaluated the message by how practically relevant and transformational, how helpful, it was for the hearers. Neither of us was interested simply in the eloquence or wit of my delivery. We wanted the message to make a positive difference in the life of every listener. I wanted every message to encourage and inspire people to become all they could be. Mary joined me by encouraging me to "go for the significant."

Success is good; no one wants to be a failure. But if dreamers settle for success, and not significance, then their dreams are too small. Each week national magazines carry articles on athletes who are successful. Their faces (and biceps) appear in commercials and on cereal boxes. But all too often those same names appear in headlines recounting the latest sports scandal. Is their success connected to anything significant?

When I think of professional basketball player A. C. Green, I see both success and significance. Through Athletes for Abstinence, Green and fellow athletes call young people to higher standards of sexual purity, respect for themselves, and respect for others than the world generally expects from them. A. C. Green and football stars Reggie White, Darrell Green, and Barry Sanders, basketball star David Robinson, decathlete Dave Johnson, and rap recording star Idol King recorded a video entitled "It Ain't Worth It" to pass their message on to young people.

Sharing a common vision, these men—dream makers for one another—are not simply successful in terms of fame and fortune; they encourage others to lives of significance. They each have found another dream mate who encourages them in their individual lives to maintain high standards, even when the rest of the world seems to expect far less. The dream mate who stands beside them unfailingly is God. Darrell Green speaks for all of them when he states, "We think we have the power of God to help us stand alone" advocating a significant cause.[5]

Look for a dream mate dedicated to helping you find significance in yourself and in your dream. The best place to start your search for a dream mate who will call you to significance is with God.

RESPONDS TO YOUR IDEAS WITH RESPECT

A DREAM MATE RESPONDS to your ideas with respect. Ideas are seeds of significance. Every great dream begins with the seed of an idea. If ideas are discarded before they have a chance to push their way through the soil—to be investigated and tested—the possibility of a fruitful dream is lost forever. Dream mates will help you explore, investigate, and test your ideas.

A word of caution: Not every idea is a good idea. For some ideas, we need a dream mate who loves us enough to say, "That's hooey." If the idea is harmful, selfish, or evil, we need to be told the truth—in love, with respect. Distinguishing between what is helpful and what isn't can be difficult. For that reason, we need to sift every idea through the screen of significance.

EXPECTS THE BEST

A DREAM MATE EXPECTS the best for you and from you. The students at Carlmont High had chewed up and spit out every teacher sent to teach them, until Louanne Johnson took a tough, persistent, patient, positive approach.

On Louanne's first day on the job, as she wrote her name on the blackboard, a hardcover dictionary slammed into the board only inches from her head. Drawing on her training as a Marine and on her own inner reserves, Louanne calmly continued writing her name, then turned around to face the defiant teen who had thrown the book.

Pointedly instructing him to sit down, she announced, "I'm too young to retire and too mean to quit. You're stuck with me."

In the five years to follow, Louanne Johnson would turn around the lives of those kids. That first day she told the students that every one of them started with an "A" in her class. Most of them had never in their lives received an "A." Louanne went on to tell them that they had a choice: They could either keep the "A," or lose it.

Combining the nothing-but-your-best expectations of a boot-camp sergeant (demeaning slurs meant immediate dismissal from her class) with liberal rewards for achievement (such as tossing out candy bars for correct answers), she believed in her students when no one else would. When one student told her he wouldn't do homework because his friends would ridicule him, Johnson let him turn his assignments in secretly so he wouldn't lose face. That young man went on to become a technician in a scientific laboratory, and his was not an isolated story of achievement.[6]

Louanne Johnson, the inspiration for the movie *Dangerous Minds*, was a dream mate for her students, standing by them with patience, perseverance, and positive faith. Every dreamer needs someone who expects the best from, and for, them.

AFFIRMS YOUR TALENTS AND ABILITIES

A DREAM MATE AFFIRMS your talents and abilities. Affirmation is like rocket fuel for great dreams and dreamers. The space shuttle's tanks need to be filled with both solid and liquid fuel to power a successful launch, flight, and landing. Dream mates continually fill the dreamer's tanks with affirming actions and words. We hear a lot about taking affirmative action to help solve some of the world's complicated problems. Affirmative actions keep the engines burning once the dream has been ignited. Affirmative words fuel a dreamer's heart with joy and enthusiasm.

Dream mates point out a dreamer's strengths and gifts. Certainly they acknowledge weaknesses, but they do it in a constructive, productive way that does not tear down the dream or the dreamer. If the people closest to you seem to make a career out of criticizing or pointing out your faults and flaws, of putting you down, then you need to look outside that circle for a friend, a teacher, a mentor, a counselor, or a supporting group of people who will speak to you the truth of who you are in positive, strengthening ways.

When you choose a dream mate, think in terms of someone who has a positive orientation. There was a person on my church board when I first arrived at Joy who was a self-proclaimed "opposer." This person told me he or she would vote against everything presented in order to keep me honest. This kind of person is not a candidate to be the trustee of a dream. I am not suggesting that you find only people who always agree with everything you say or do, but look for people who are in favor of improvement, motivation, and positive possibilities.

Dream mates need to be innovative in their caregiving, and creative—but genuine—in their compliments. The key is to recognize, and to look for meaningful ways to affirm, the dreamer's God-given talents and abilities.

MAXIMIZES LEARNING AND GROWTH OPPORTUNITIES TO IMPROVE THE DREAM

A DREAM MATE MAXIMIZES learning and growth opportunities to improve the dream. Dream mates encourage the dreamer to continually refine and improve the dream.

A favorite phrase of driver's education instructors is "Don't look at the car in front of you. Look *ahead of* the car in front of you." Looking farther down the road helps drivers see potential hazards— such things as brake lights on cars out ahead—and adjust their speed and driving accordingly before the problem is in their face. Like a driving instructor, a good dream mate encourages a dreamer to stay alert and look beyond today's challenge.

In an earlier chapter, I mentioned the bowling coach telling a young boy to set his feet straight ahead and then keep his eyes on the arrows on the lane ahead of him. Dream mates act as that kind of coach—challenging dreamers to assess where they are and to look ahead, to develop new strategies, and to push for excellence.

No dream, or dreamer, is perfect. All dreamers need to learn and grow and "fine tune" their dreams as they live them out. Dream mates need to look for and help maximize improvement opportunities.

MAKES THE MOST OF MISTAKES AND FAILURES

JAZZ MUSICIAN MILES DAVIS said, "Do not fear mistakes—there are none." That's good advice for dreamers and dream mates. You see, a dream mate makes the most of mistakes and failures. Important dreams are accomplished by dreamers who make the most of all their mistakes and failures. When a dreamer makes a mistake or experiences failure, a dream mate does well to ask "What?" and not "How?" By that I mean, "How did that happen?" is not a helpful question. "How" focuses on the problem. It's best to focus on *what*—as in "What did you learn? What are you going to do next?"—because *what* focuses on the solution.

> *♪♪*
>
> **Dream mates challenge dreamers to assess where they are and to look ahead, to develop new strategies, and to push for excellence.**

It has been said that failure, when not used profitably, quickly solidifies and turns a heart to lead, making *action* very difficult. After my first year as the pastor of Community Church of Joy, about half of the two hundred members were so upset with changes I had made to make the church more practical, relevant, and fresh, that they left the church. I really felt like a failure! I made plenty of mistakes, but I didn't just sit at home, stew, or complain. I committed myself to work toward turning around my failures.

One of the first things I did was call a dream mate, a pastor I really admired: Dr. Lloyd Ogilvie, who is now chaplain of the U.S. Senate. I laid out my problem and asked for his advice and help. Dr. Ogilvie counseled me to build on my mistakes and failures. He told me to find meaningful ways to let every person in my little congregation know how much I loved and appreciated them. He recommended that I give people hugs and write notes of encouragement so as to create a warm, loving, caring, friendly atmosphere where love could grow. Lloyd said, "When love grows, dreams will grow."

I went back to my church the next Sunday determined to stand by the door when people left and give everybody a hug. For me this was a stretch, because I grew up in a climate that did not encourage public demonstrations of affection. Well, that morning the first person out the door was a bearded, burly man who was vocally opposed to my leadership. As I reached out to hug him, I was sure he was going to punch me. Thankfully, he just grunted and rushed off. Most of the people joyfully received the warm gesture and shared their own hugs with one another. God used my change of attitude to kindle a more inviting, friendly environment, and the church started to "grow in love" as well as in size.

I am glad I listened to Lloyd Ogilvie! With a dream mate's help, and with the help of other dream mates, the congregation has continued to grow. The two hundred members have multiplied a hundredfold, several times over. Learning how to make the most of a mistake keeps the dream growing.

Find a dream mate today who will help you make the most of your mistakes and failures.

ACCEPTS ONLY EXCELLENCE

A DREAM MATE CALLS us to excellence. Mediocrity is disastrous. My mother, who was a special dream mate, used to repeat the familiar rhyme:

Good, better, best—
Never let it rest
Until your good is better
And your better is best!

It is always important to insist on excellence. Excellence is more than doing things right; excellence is doing the right things, as well

51

as doing things right. It is impossible for dreamers to live out their dreams excellently by doing wrong things, even if they are done in the right way. An excellent dream mate helps keep the dreamer's conscience right and the dream on the right course to ensure excellence.

Think in terms of the NASA space program. For a spacecraft traveling from the earth to the moon, an error of only half a degree in course would cause a "miss." Forget a bull's-eye landing; the craft would miss the moon entirely. If the target were smaller than the moon—for instance, an orbital window of ten miles—a difference of some .002 degrees in course would cause a miss. Imagine how precise the navigation must be to land a craft at a specific moon site!

To maintain a true—an excellent—course takes a team effort. The movie *Apollo 13* made this clear on many levels. That voyage seemed doomed at stage after stage. And finally, having successfully overcome the life-threatening problems of recharging the reentry batteries and "jury-rigging" carbon dioxide scrubbers, the crew faced the ominous problem of aligning the guidance computer that would enable the crew to navigate safely back to earth.

Proper alignment of the guidance computer was essential. Any error in alignment could cause the craft to miss the earth or burn up on reentry. And yet the spacecraft was traveling in a cloud of debris from the exploded oxygen tank—debris that sparkled in the sun, making it impossible for the astronauts to sight crucial star markers.

What saved the day? Some years earlier, a NASA engineer had envisioned just such a problem. He had programmed into the ground guidance computers a way to use the earth's terminator line—the boundary between the earth's illuminated and dark hemispheres—and the sun as reference points. These were reference points the *Apollo* crew could see even through the debris. This almost forgotten program was remembered in time to avert disaster.

A dream mate, like *Apollo 13*'s NASA teammates, can supply new reference points when a dreamer's own vision is obscured, providing the midcourse corrections needed to keep the dream and the dreamer on a true and excellent course.

TAKES TIME TO GIVE HONEST FEEDBACK

A DREAM MATE TAKES time to give honest feedback. There are two key elements in this profile point: *time* and *feedback*. Let's look at them separately.

My friend Tim tells me that time is the new money. He is correct: Time is a valuable treasure. Dreamers need a dream mate who is willing to spend their valuable time to give honest feedback. Great dreams and dreamers are worth this investment. Dream mates need to take the time required to show that what is honest should have a higher value than what is popular. A solid dream mate will be willing to risk being misunderstood by being honest.

Scheduling dream time can be challenging. All of us have important demands on our time. That is why it is good to plan a weekly, monthly, quarterly, or yearly time when you share one another's dreams. For some of my dream mates, we simply call once a month to talk about dream difficulties and delights. We give some feedback but mostly listen.

> Dream mates are God's messengers of encouragement to help dreamers hang in and hang tough until the dream comes true.

With other dream mates I schedule a weekly lunch. The agenda is quite relaxed and informal. But our time together encourages both the dream and dreamer.

There are still other dream mates I strategize with once a year. We block out three or four hours and discuss our dreams.

The one dream mate I check in with almost daily is my wife. We value and honor each other's dreams so much that we are willing to take whatever time it takes to "dream talk" and "dream shop."

When dreamers don't get honest feedback, dreams are likely to derail, digress, and diminish. Dreamers need to know the facts, the realities, and the possibilities in order to realize their dreams, and dream mates help by giving honest feedback.

Honest feedback requires a "fearless" evaluation of what attitudes and actions are moving the dreamer toward the dream, and what is slowing progress, diverting it, or bringing the dream to a sudden halt. Often dream mates can give a more accurate, objective assessment than can the dreamers themselves because their emotional fears are not in the way, clouding judgment. Wise dream mates can help remove a dreamer's fear of the evaluation process. This is not achieved by condemnation or criticism, but by helping the dreamer maximize abilities and opportunities, thus moving more effectively and efficiently toward realizing the dream.

ENCOURAGES YOU CONTINUALLY AND CREATIVELY

A DREAM MATE ENCOURAGES you, not based on your performance, but continually and creatively, to help you persevere. Great dreamers persevere. That isn't easy. In fact, without unconditional, nonjudgmental encouragement from a dedicated dream mate, it is all too easy for a dreamer to quit. How many dreams have never been realized because the dreamer quit?

Winston Churchill is famous for his words "Never quit. Never, never, never quit." This is much easier to say than to do. Persevering when everything in a dreamer wants to say, "That's enough! I've had it! I can't continue! I'm finished," is almost impossible without the help of a dream mate who responds, "Go for it! You can do it! I believe in you! It's possible! Keep on!" Dream mates are God's messengers of encouragement to help dreamers hang in and hang tough until the dream comes true.

PRACTICAL POINTERS

GREAT DREAMS HAVE THE potential of drawing in the support and energy of many people—a dream network or dream team. And who doesn't want to be part of a winning team?

Stop at this point and contemplate people you know who already are, or could be, good dream mates. Think about what you've already read and also reflect on these points:

- Consider people who dare to think big.
- Surround yourself with attitudes of possibility.
- Look for people with enthusiasm.
- Seek people with discernment who are ethical, moral, and trustworthy.
- Find people who genuinely respect the worth of every individual.

Write or speak to others who have achieved a dream and ask for their advice and input. Take time right now to write down your top ten dream mates—or candidates. Give each one a call or write and invite him or her to share in a dream adventure of a lifetime. Why not in turn offer yourself as a dream mate?

NO ONE NEEDS TO DREAM ALONE

DURING A DINNER CONVERSATION, Robert Schuller told me about a powerfully touching experience in South Africa, where he was addressing some of the greatest black leaders in the world. As he stood before the group after being introduced, Bob just looked into the eyes of these men and women who had suffered so much for so long. He suddenly "lost" his prepared speech. What could he possibly say that would make a difference? Why had he been asked to speak? What did he have to say?

In the silence, those surrounding Bob saw tears flowing from his eyes. He couldn't speak, but he could cry.

One man in the group stood up and walked toward Bob, who was feeling pretty awkward by this time. The man said, "Dr. Schuller, among our people we will not let anyone cry alone." With that, tears poured from the eyes of that man—and others.

This is the kind of passion and partnership that the best of all dream mates can provide. You are a most fortunate dreamer if you find someone who will stick by you—who helps you carry your joys and your setbacks, who wants the best for you, who encourages you to live to your full potential.

Whether or not you find "the ultimate" loyal, wise, compassionate, human dream mate, I encourage you to turn to one dream mate who has proven to me to be reliable and trustworthy beyond my imagination. My most trusted dream mate is Jesus Christ, who goes before me to show the way, walks beside me to befriend me, stands behind me to encourage me, hovers over me to watch me, and lives within me to fill me with peace. God will go the distance with us.

I speak with confidence because I know that he gives me precisely what I *need* instead of simply what I *want*. My dream wants are generated from my limited human understanding. Settling for what I want will never ultimately satisfy me.

Over the last ten years, I have tried to envision what a twenty-first-century irresistible, inspirational television program would be like. As I initially prayed about the vision, I sensed that I should wait.

Then, this last September, a consultant told me it was time for Community Church of Joy to develop a weekly television program. God had told me to wait, and now, ten years from the time I first glimpsed the vision, the consultant said it was time to pursue the dream. After hearing those words of encouragement to launch the dream, in my mind I started to pull together what the program would look like. Emotionally I felt ready; spiritually I felt a confident peace. Now as I pursue this dream, at every corner the lights are green. The only explanation for these open doors is that my most trusted dream mate, Jesus Christ, is going before me to show the way.

Jesus is the captain of my dream team, but over the years there have been many other dream mates playing alongside me. When Community Church of Joy has faced major decisions, Dr. Lloyd Ogilvie and Dr. Lyle Schaller have always been readily available with wise counsel. Dr. Robert Schuller is one of my greatest encouragers. My parents always treated my dreams with respect. When my family would sit around the dinner table, my wife and children would listen to my dreams. Sometimes they'd say "That's crazy!" but most often they'd affirm "That's exciting!" When you have teammates like that, you can't lose.

Knowing that Christ wants what is best for my present and future, I trust his judgment and guidance. He has all the wisdom and knowledge I search for. He also has the incredible power to do more than I could ever do. That's exactly what we need for all our dreams to come true.

> **You will always have a dream mate when you include God in your dreams.**

This prayer, attributed to St. Patrick, gives a call that challenges each of us to listen for the word of God as he speaks to our dreams—directly to our spirit, through his Word, or through a "friend or stranger" who is a dream mate. You will always have a dream mate when you include God in your dreams.

Christ be with me, Christ within me,
Christ behind me, Christ before me,
Christ beside me, Christ to win me,
Christ to comfort and restore me,
Christ beneath me, Christ above me,
Christ in quiet, Christ in danger,
Christ in mouth of friend or stranger.

Four

The Dynamic Dream Equation

O NE OF LIFE'S PARADOXICAL principles is that the whole is often greater than the sum of its parts. This holds true for awakening our dreams. Consider the following formula, which I call the dynamic dream equation:

TALENT + GOD'S CALL + PREPARATION + OPPORTUNITY = WAKING UP YOUR DREAM

In this chapter, we'll examine the elements of the dynamic dream equation one by one to learn why each is necessary in laying a solid foundation for living out God-inspired dreams.

DISCOVERING TALENT

GOD GIVES EVERYONE DIFFERENT, but tremendous, talents. Your talents are different from mine, each of us being uniquely created. Even if a dream is a good one—not a scheme—it may not be the "best" dream for us, considering our God-given talents. We need discernment to determine whether we have the talents and abilities required to realize our dreams. It's easy to settle for something good, only to miss out on the better.

An early lesson in discovering my talents came for me when, as a teenager, I dreamed of being a professional athlete. I was athletically adequate, but not exceptional. Discovering that I was not exceptionally talented in athletics helped me make the choice not to follow that dream. I also dreamed of becoming a professional musician. Even though I pushed my talent "to the max," I was just a good musician, not a great one. I realized that pursuing a career in either professional music or athletics was not the best use for my life.

Identifying talent is especially critical for young people, who may not know their own deeply imbedded God-given talents. This is one place where a dream mate can be very helpful—having someone who believes in and respects you and helps you sort *the good* from the *better* or *best*.

We walk a fine line in discovering and nurturing our talents, so we need to elicit credible feedback from others. At the same time, I caution you never to permit one person's disappointment to cancel your appointment with pursuing your dreams. Just as surely as the slightest bit of egg yolk, slipped in with the egg whites, spells death for a meringue, one simple comment that plants doubts in your mind can impair the entire dreaming process. If a teacher, parent, friend, or work associate tells you that you don't have what it takes, don't automatically accept that opinion as fact.

> A dream mate is someone who believes in and respects you, and helps you sort *the good* from the *better* or *best*.

All of us know people who have developed mental excellence, effectiveness, and efficiency even in the face of other people's doubts about their capabilities. Fortunately my friend Peter Daniels didn't let other people's doubts interfere with his dreams. Mrs. Phillips, his fourth-grade teacher, told Peter he was no good and would never amount to anything, but Peter wasn't willing to believe that. Although he remained illiterate until he was twenty-six years old, Peter kept feeding on a steady diet of hope, courage, and persistence. Today Peter is one of the most successful business leaders in all of

Australia. The man who couldn't read now reads at least one book every week.

And consider the life story of one talented speaker: James Earl Jones. From the age of eight, Jones had a stuttering problem so severe that the only way his teachers could measure his progress was to have him write out his lessons. Although he could speak to the animals on his grandparents' farm, he just froze when he was introduced to new people or when he tried to read aloud.

When James was fourteen, an English teacher, Donald Crouch, discovered that James loved to read and write poetry—though he refused to read his poems aloud in class. With wisdom and insight, Crouch challenged James to prove that he had truly written one of his poems by reciting it from memory. James stood trembling, facing the mocking grins of his classmates, and then began to recite—and continued reciting his poem smoothly to the end.

James Earl Jones had a God-given talent that was buried until a teacher went hunting for it. With encouragement, James recited more poetry; he eventually entered debates and speech contests, and the boy who couldn't speak began to dream of a career as an actor, like his father. Crouch encouraged James to go on to college, and he won a scholarship to the University of Michigan.[1]

If you suspect you have talent in an area, explore it. Find avenues to try out your abilities, then assess the results objectively and honestly. Don't dismiss the idea after only one trial—keep going.

HEARING GOD'S CALL

IT'S A MISCONCEPTION THAT dreams come from "lightning bolts" or massive flares of insight. That may occasionally happen but, most often, the greatest dreams come from a tiny spark, like the small ember that burned within Carol Porter's heart.

Carol, a registered nurse in Houston, Texas, was deeply shaken when a baby she had helped deliver was brought to the hospital just a few months later, dead from malnutrition. Something began to burn within Carol. Later, when she and her husband, Hurt, saw children from an apartment complex next door to a fast-food restaurant eating out of the restaurant's dumpster, Carol knew she had to do something. In 1984, Carol's mother, Lula Doe, had persuaded a local supermarket not to throw out its blemished produce, but to let her distribute it to the poor. Drawing inspiration from her mother, Carol and Hurt simply began to do the same.

They solicited surplus food from markets, prepared it at their own home, and distributed it to homeless people living under bridges and to children in community centers. From this modest beginning, Kid-Care was born. Carol and Hurt quit their jobs and created what amounts to the country's first meals-on-wheels program for hungry children. The Porters' home became Kid-Care's kitchen where, by 1994, Carol, Hurt, and nearly 50 volunteers turned out 38,000 meals a month to give 14,000 hungry children two meals a day: a brown-bag lunch and one hot meal.

Kid-Care's annual budget has grown to $500,000, coming from some corporate contributions and, primarily, from individual donations made possible by Carol's unflagging enthusiasm and effort. Hurt draws a modest stipend of $2,000 a month, and Carol takes no salary at all. Carol and Hurt now dream of "seeding" Kid-Care groups in other cities. When people ask what's in it for them, Carol replies, "I tell them to go the route with me and see my kids' faces. That's what's in it for me."[2]

Lives are being changed because Carol Porter responded to that small ember that burned within her. If your dream is part of God's call for you, it won't be a "flash in the pan" that flares up only to burn out just as quickly; the dream will still be there every morning, glowing and growing within you.

God calls us, everyone, to a life-fulfilling dream. It may be to teach or to drive a truck, to be a doctor or a homemaker, to be a gardener, an engineer, an actor, or a minister. Whatever God desires, he will inspire within us.

God Speaks Through His Word

HOW DO WE GET to know God's dreams? The first step is to get to know God through the Bible. In chapter 2, I mentioned the biblical measure: In one way or another our dreams should result in our loving God and loving people. If either the result or process of pursuing your dream would contradict that principle, you can be assured that God's call is not behind the dream. God's call will always line up with his Word.

God Speaks to Our Spirit

PAY ATTENTION TO YOUR intuition. Intuition comes from an informed and prepared subconscious level. It is an awareness that comes without conscious attention or reason, but it does involve processing something perceived or learned. In that way, it differs from simple wishful thinking. Dreams formed in your heart today can emerge in your head tomorrow.

God Speaks Through Uncertainty

BUT A SENSE OF tension within us sometimes accompanies our dreams. Be careful not to take the anxiety that comes from uncertainty too lightly; it may be the harbinger of God's creative, innovative will. Tension can arise when there is a conflict between our own desire to "go" and an undefined anxiety that seems to say "no." That anxiety may be God's word to your spirit that the dream is not of God, that it may be a Godly dream but not for you, or that the time is not yet right to act on the dream. This tension is positive when healthy stirrings in our souls force us to look deeper into what really matters. When I am struggling most, I know I am walking on the springboard that will lift me to new levels of discovery and clearer discernment of my dreams.

Jimmy Carter describes the creative possibility of anxiety when it arises from "the absence of satisfaction for the way things are." Anxiety is not something to be avoided, he suggests, if it produces in us the kind of creative tension that results in inspiration, challenge, and a concern to know more than we already know.[3]

Walt Disney used anxious uncertainty well. He shared his dreams, presenting them to family, friends, and board members. Often everyone would violently oppose the dream. After considering the tension that opposition produced, if Disney still believed a dream should be done, he would get it done. Many times, in fact, if the dream didn't face unanimous opposition, Walt would scrap the idea, thinking it might not be a dream important enough to invest his life in.

Responding to God's Call

TOM LEHMAN, ONE OF the top ten money winners in professional golf over the last several years, believes God created and called him to be one of the very best golfers in the world. Tom possessed talent, as well as motivation, that led him often to be the last person left on the course, practicing in darkness and icy rains.

Tom entered—and lost—his first tournament, then the next, and the next as well. At one point, he was out of money and almost out of hope. On his knees in prayer one night, at a time when he felt most lonely and defeated, Tom sensed that God was affirming his call to be a professional golfer. The next day, Tom hit the greens again. He won the qualifying round of one tournament and went on to win a sizable prize. Tom gave God the credit for that success and for all the others since then.

What mattered to Tom was not the size of the dividend but the source of his dream. God's call to carry through on the dream to become a great golfer gave Tom the courage, confidence, and commitment he needed to persevere.

We may have talent, but without God's call, our dreams will lack the transcending potential and power that produces a life that is a dream come true. The movie *Chariots of Fire* was based on the life of British Olympic runner Eric Liddel, an athlete clearly dedicated to a significant dream of serving God with his whole life. In the movie, Liddel says, "God made me fast, and when I run, it gives God pleasure."

You and I have a choice: We can pursue our own dreams, or we can pursue God's dreams. Our own dreams can be tantalizing, and through them we can accomplish good things, but, ultimately, God's dreams are the dreams that can satisfy our longing to influence our own corner of the world for the best.

Canadian poet Henry Drummond observed that, after all is said and done, the greatest thing anyone can achieve is to have done the will of God. If you feel God's call, keep going. God can—and does—speak as we move out and take the next step.

MAKING PREPARATIONS

ADDED TO TALENT AND call is preparation. Talent needs to be continually polished through preparation, and that preparation process lasts a lifetime. Preparation calls for planning, practicing, and anticipating obstacles. Preparation does not mean we will know what lies ahead, but we can anticipate what might be ahead and equip ourselves for it.

> *ॐ*
>
> **You and I have a choice: We can pursue our own dreams, or we can pursue God's dreams.**

Whether in family life, at work, or in pursuing your dream, it is important to follow the motto of the Boy Scouts: "Be prepared." Preparation is not an easy task. I see it this way: An ounce of preparation equals a pound of perspiration!

As we plan, study, practice, and improve our abilities, we prepare ourselves to capture our dreams. The College Entrance Examination Board, which for years maintained that SAT preparation courses did nothing to improve students' scores on the Scholastic Assessment Test, now sells computer software to help students prepare for the test. A number of studies report that students make average gains of 80 to 160 points through SAT coaching courses.

As you prepare to "go for" your dream, think in terms of a game plan. What are you going to need to get to your end goal? During my first year as the minister of Community Church of Joy, I spent my dream day designing one-, three-, five-, and ten-year strategic plans. I envisioned vivid pictures of real people—with real needs, hurts, and problems, and with hopeful, healthy possibilities. I tried to imagine the best ways to help and encourage them.

Those imaginings became a concrete plan that I wrote down in careful detail. Then I shared those ideas with other people, honing and refining them until the ideas became meaningful programs and processes. Eighteen years ago, filled with faith and armed with determination, I made those plans. And yes—those plans were fulfilled.

I have heard it said that many obstacles to realizing a dream are removed when one learns the difference between motion and direction. I'm reminded of a *Peanuts* cartoon I once saw by that master of succinct truth Charles Schulz. Lucy tells Charlie Brown that she's decided to begin a new hobby. Charlie Brown commends her decision, saying how important it is to accomplish something meaningful with your life. Lucy's incredulous response was, roughly, "Accomplish something? I thought all we were supposed to do was keep busy!"

We may keep busy going through motions that seem to be living out our dreams, but if we don't have the clear direction that comes from clear planning, we may never realize our dreams. Making plans with reasonable, accountable actions helps us to manage our time, energy, and ideas more effectively and more efficiently. Wise planning allows us to capture the dream.

Sound planning often involves breaking our dream down into smaller, more manageable steps. Small incremental dreams are like navigational reference points that keep us on track. A friend of mine was a navigator in the Air Force in the days before the wide use of inertial navigation systems. He tells me that in daylight, flying over land was no problem; pilots could take their bearings from roads and other landmarks on the ground. But flying over the ocean was a different story. With no land markings, the navigator could determine the plane's position only by taking careful sextant sightings of the sun, moon, planets, and stars. The navigator's readings helped the pilots correct their course to keep heading toward their destination.

If his "fixes" were off, the aircraft's final destination was far from its intended destination. Without accurate reference points from which a pilot could periodically take his bearings, he and the crew could circle aimlessly over open water and never find a landing strip.

These smaller, incremental dreams function as reference points to help us navigate a true course, rather than wandering aimlessly across all the unknowns of life. They help us alter our course when we need to; dream by dream we keep moving toward our desired destination—the ultimate dream we want to come true.

> Dreamers should prepare to achieve a dream by assessing and making plans to acquire three essentials: energy, equipment, and education.

I propose that any dreamer seek—prepare—to achieve a dream by assessing and making plans to acquire three essentials: energy, equipment, and education. Ask yourself these three important questions:

S   What do I need to do to increase my *stamina* and
E   *energy* to allow me to capture my dream?
E   In what *equipment* do I need to invest resources or creativity to achieve my dream?
K   What do I need to *know*?

Planning for Stamina and Energy

TO WORK FOR AND live out their dreams at their optimal levels, dreamers need to be physically sound and prepared to expend the extra energy that living out the dream will require. When you are tired or out of shape, poorly nourished, or poorly prepared, it becomes difficult to care about finding or living out your dreams.

Eating a well-balanced, nutritionally sensible diet is basic physical preparation for any dreamer, and many good books exist outlining sound dietary guidelines. Ask your doctor or a dietitian if you have questions regarding what is right for you, and decide to follow sensible guidelines in what you eat. It does make a difference in terms of your strength, health, and even your outlook.

Good dreams can die when dreamers lack energy. I say that and I also admit that there's something circular about dreaming and physical energy. Energy fuels dreams and dreams can fuel physical activity.

Here's what I mean: When I arrived at Community Church of Joy, I was physically out of shape. I woke up tired. I went to bed tired. After a day's work, I had no energy left to play with my children or enjoy time with my wife. I had no energy to work to carry out my dreams, no energy to dream new dreams. One day, the thought struck me that the energy to dream is created by exercise. In fact, my body was crying out for exercise.

I decided to solve my physical dilemma—my dream dilemma— by getting up thirty minutes earlier to jog. After jogging one block, I was exhausted, but I kept going. As I ran, I dreamed of shaping up into excellent physical condition. My stamina increased. It took me months to accomplish, but the payoff was valuable. Getting into good physical condition benefited my family, my congregation, myself, and my dreaming capacity.

My physical preparation led to capturing a greater dream: to run in the Fiesta Bowl Marathon. Preparing for that goal, I spent months jogging the proper daily distances, getting appropriate rest, and eating the correct diet.

In 1983, I was ready to run the race. The night before the race, friends who were coaching me told me to eat at the Spaghetti Company and load up on carbohydrates, which provide sustained energy for the body; eating right is like putting the proper fuel in the tank of a well-tuned engine. All of the preparation paid off. I successfully finished the grueling 26.2-mile course. Continuing to exercise has paid continuing benefits. When I went in for a physical recently, I passed the treadmill cardiac test with flying colors.

As you prepare for any dream, determine what physical preparations you will need to get where you want to go. Friends of mine prepared themselves physically for the strenuous hike into Havasu Canyon, one of the most unexpectedly beautiful spots in Arizona. Tucked in a narrow canyon carved into an arid plateau, Havasu Creek spills over craggy ledges to cascade into blue-green travertine pools below, giving life to a lush profusion of cottonwoods, willows, watercress and ferns, hummingbirds, warblers, canyon wrens, and lizards. My friends' dream was to walk the eleven-mile dusty descent through ruddy sandstone and rusty-streaked, buff-colored limestone walls to reach the creek.

To prepare for the trip, they practiced—by this I mean that well in advance of their trip they regularly walked carrying partially loaded backpacks. One hiking friend was particularly intent on preparing physically for the canyon hike because she has trouble with one knee; for her, the steep grades were going to be a real challenge. "I knew my struggle would be as much mental as physical," she related, "and it was. The last mile of the trail is steep switchbacks. I was tired, and my knee hurt, and I didn't even want to hear my husband's encouraging words that the end was in sight. It was in sight, all right, but a long way up! One thought kept discouragement at bay and kept me going: *I know I can take this next step.* I repeated that, every step, for a mile, and I made it to the top."

We'll talk more about the critical connection between dreams and attitudes in the next chapter, but here I briefly note that a positive mental attitude influences one's health and physical energy. Dr. Robert Andra, in a study at the Centers for Disease Control in Atlanta, looked at a random sampling of three thousand people; he found that the incidence of heart attacks nearly doubled in a group that ranked highest in feelings of hopelessness, compared with people who reported low or no feelings of hopelessness.[4]

In 1974, the work of Dr. Robert Alder of the University of Rochester suggested that the nervous system and the immune system are intricately, intimately connected. And a recent study from the Institute of Neurobiology in Rome shows a possible link between the brain and the immune system in the increase of a protein that helps neurons survive under stress. Findings such as these indicate that there is a complex link between emotion, mind, and health; this link has even given rise to a new field of inquiry—with the incredible name *psychoneuroimmunology*.

Other studies suggest that mindset matters in terms of health. When a group of 122 men who had suffered one heart attack were evaluated on their scale of optimism or pessimism, researchers found that, eight years later, twenty-one of the twenty-five most pessimistic men had died; only six of the twenty-five most optimistic had died.[5]

Ralph Waldo Emerson wisely declared, "A man is what he thinks about all day long." Norman Vincent Peale constantly preached about the power of positive attitudes. When it comes to "planning for energy," our attitudes, thoughts, emotions, and physical beings are all interconnected.

Planning for Equipment

MY FRIENDS WHO HIKED Havasu Canyon made physical preparations—they practiced—but that's not all they did. They determined what equipment they would need to capture the dream. They assessed the situation: Searing summer temperatures in the canyon often reach triple digits. Planning to hike in June, my friends went prepared for warm weather, including bathing suits and sunblock. But they also realized that northern Arizona summers can be unpredictable, so in their backpacks they carried jeans, sweatshirts, and rain ponchos.

Though it was sunny and hot the day they started their trek, on the second day it rained. One couple in their hiking party had brought no tent, so they were forced to huddle in a cave in the canyon wall. The temperature dropped, the winds rose; no one else in the party had brought anything warmer than a T-shirt. On the day they hiked out, the temperature had dropped to forty degrees and the rain turned to sleet at the top of the trail. Unlike the other hikers, my friends were dry and warm and able to enjoy the spectacular natural wonder they had dreamed of seeing. They were able to do so because they had anticipated the possibility of changing weather and committed themselves to carrying the extra equipment needed to be prepared for those changes.

In short, my friends looked at their dream, determined what equipment they would need, assessed what they had, and acquired what they still needed. At one planning stage, they saw a need for warm but lightweight sleep protection. Setting out to solve this problem, they created a layered blanket "sandwich" that was lighter and more versatile than their sleeping bags. They prevented disaster by being prepared.

When I first came to Joy, I saw some immediate needs to help meet goals for that first year: office equipment to improve communication with the congregation, garden implements to hack down the waist-high weeds and improve the appearance of the church property, more tables and chairs, and a sound system. Since I wasn't fully familiar with what equipment would best meet our needs in each of these areas, I enlisted knowledgeable dream mates to help me make decisions. Look for well-informed people with experience in the area of your needs; they can be insightful, invaluable dream mates.

Planning for Education

"WHAT DO I NEED to know?" What new skills might you need to capture your dream? By its very nature, a dream calls us to stretch our capacities. For some dreams, that "stretch" is nearly all physical. But most dreams require that we learn some new skill or knowledge and extend ourselves mentally. Our mental capacity is incredible. Our minds have practically unlimited potential and possibilities. To a dreamer, the mind is a magnificent gift. We use only a small percentage of its capacity. The possibilities are endless.

To know what new knowledge you need, you'll have to get acquainted with the circumstances that surround your dream opportunity. For example, people whose dream is financial independence will need to dig out information—anything they can find about investments and ways to set aside money—so that, when the right opportunity comes along, they are ready to act.

Planning for education may or may not involve going back to school. For me—deciding to switch careers and become a minister—capturing the dream required formal education. I'd had four years of college, but I had to plan for four years of seminary. Later, I saw the value of pursuing a doctorate in theology. For some time, that dream kept being pushed aside by the demands of my job and my lack of finances. Finally I made the commitment to fill out the application. Then I enrolled in my first class. Searching for the money I needed was a great adventure. It took great patience, persistence, and prayer, but I found it. In that process, I discovered there are people looking for a place where their money can make a positive difference.

Then, only three short years later, I finished my classes, wrote my dissertation, and completed the dream of earning my doctorate. Effective planning is driven by three things: a dream, a desire, and determination.

How can you plan for and go for the knowledge you'll need to capture your dream? Consider these practical suggestions:

1. Read regularly. Subscribe to journals that will keep you up to date.
2. Attend seminars, classes, and workshops.
3. Listen to enriching audio or video tapes often.
4. Network with people who have experience.

The planning we've talked about here is not a one-shot deal. What some call "carbo-loading"—preparing for the race—is a life-long process. In terms of achieving our dreams, we should be careful to load up on those things that will strengthen and enhance our capacities. To be dependably effective, preparation should be a consistent routine, not a drastic cram session.

Planning with Flexibility

IT IS ESSENTIAL TO PLAN *for* stamina and energy, equipment, and knowledge to fully realize our dreams, but it is also important in all these areas to plan *with* flexibility. Develop a contingency plan. A contingency plan is not a "back-*out*," but a "back*up*" plan. Having backup is a positive step that looks for a way in; backing out is a negative step that looks for a way out. Find alternate ways through which your dream can become a reality.

When we bought the land where our Community Church of Joy would be developed, we considered a contingency plan. In buying the land for $25,000 an acre, we knew that within a year it would be worth at least that much, if not more. It was, indeed, appraised at $30,000 an acre. We knew we could sell the land and use the profits to purchase another property if we were unable to raise the money to build our project. We also decided to put enough money aside to make the mortgage payment for two years, just in case we didn't have the cash flow to meet the $25,000-per-month payment. Backing up your dream ensures against having to back out of it.

Be flexible. In the case of Community Church of Joy's dream, through preparation we have been more alert and able to adapt to changes. Change is a given, but if we are prepared for change, we can deal with its pressures and better plan for what should be done next. Considering possible scenarios before they happen ensures that important decisions will not have to be "seat of the pants" or "off the cuff" decisions.

A recent example illustrates this principle. A high school football team found themselves with a fourth down and eleven yards to go. They were deep in their own territory—in fact, they were on their own two-yard line, facing 98 yards to go for a touchdown. The opposing team expected a punt, but the punter called an audible. He changed the play to a fake punt, running (rather than punting) 35 yards down the field before his opponents brought him down. The team scored a touchdown on the next play because their opponents were still shaken by—and unprepared for—what had happened.

Stay flexible!

Evaluation is an important component of flexibility, because evaluation is the tool that tells us whether what we are doing is—or is not—producing the results we desire. Evaluation also helps us decide which of the options available to us might work best to accomplish our goal. The Japanese use a great word in their process of total quality management: _kaizen_, meaning _continuous improvement_. Continuous improvement is possible only when there is ongoing evaluation coupled with a willingness to "shift gears," if necessary, to remain on a course toward excellence. Evaluation is as important in living out our dreams as it is in business and industry!

SEIZING OPPORTUNITY

SEEING AND SEIZING OPPORTUNITY is also a must if we are to capture our dreams.

Sometimes we prepare and lay out our plans, and those very calculated plans open doors to opportunity. We simply must be ready to _recognize_ them and ready to make things happen. We have the choice to wait for things to happen or to make things happen. Dr. Wayne Dyer made his book _Your Erroneous Zones_ a bestseller by buying several hundred copies, getting in his car, and driving twenty-eight thousand miles to visit bookstores all over America, distributing and promoting his own book. It did, in fact, become a bestseller.

Sometimes, though, opportunity takes us by surprise. A person looking for opportunity must be open to _serendipity_. Horace Walpole introduced the word when he wrote about the princes of a place called Serendip, who were continually discovering things they were not looking for—thus, serendipity. Wise dreamers never pass up accidental or unintentional discoveries; they may be doorways to dreams. An example: Dr. Alexander Fleming was making some studies of bacteria, growing bacterial colonies in flat, open dishes. He was examining one of these culture plates under his microscope when he found it was contaminated with mold. Another scientist might have considered this plate ruined and thrown it away. But Fleming did not.

Upon closer examination of the plate, Fleming observed that no bacteria were growing near the mold. Struck by this surprising discovery, he reasoned that the mold might prevent the spread of bacteria. If Dr. Fleming had ignored this "something" he wasn't looking for—this serendipity—we might not have penicillin today.

We ought to be ready to recognize serendipity when it comes, but that doesn't mean we should sit and wait for the unexpected to happen. Serendipity, it has been said, accounts for perhaps 1 percent of the good things we receive in life; the other 99 percent come from hard work and effort. Serendipity is not magic. It generally occurs when we are in the act of doing something—stepping out in faith.

> ✍
>
> **Serendipity is not magic. It generally occurs when we are in the act of doing something— stepping out in faith.**

In an Old Testament account, the Hebrew people were amassed at the bank of the Jordan River, ready to enter the Promised Land. But how were they going to realize their dream—to get across the river, which was at flood stage? Their leader, Joshua, turned to God, who told him to "tell the priests who carry the ark of the covenant: 'When you reach the edge of the Jordan's waters, go and stand in the river.'" The priests weren't to stand at the river's edge and wait for a miracle; they were told to get their feet wet. *As they walked* into the river, "the water from upstream stopped flowing. It piled up in a heap a great distance away," and the people crossed on dry ground.[6] For God's intervention to occur, the people first had to get moving and get their feet wet.

The man whose name became synonymous with cookies, Wally Amos, took advantage of serendipitous events to reach his dream. Note that at each stage he kept working, looking for the next opportunity. As a young man, Amos moved from a job as a cook through a stint in the Air Force. In time, he held a job as a stock clerk for Saks Fifth Avenue, then as manager of the supply department for that store. He left and took a position with the William Morris Talent Agency, starting in the mailroom and moving up to agent within a year. As a William Morris agent, he would give his homemade cookies as a thank-you to customers, who encouraged him to market them. When Amos launched his cookie venture, two of those former customers offered not only advice but also concrete help with graphics and construction of his stands, helping Amos turn his dream into reality.

Amos notes that none of his early occupations were what he had in mind as his best dream for a career, yet each one proved to be an opportunity that served as a springboard toward what ultimately became his goal.[7]

The Bible has some good counsel about seeing and seizing opportunity: "Ask and it will be given to you; seek and you will find; knock and the door will be opened to you."[8]

The words for *ask*, *seek*, and *knock* in the original Greek are in the present imperative tense, which indicates continuous action. In other words, we are to keep on *asking* until we receive opportunity, *seeking* opportunity until we find it, *knocking* on the door of opportunity until it opens.

Jack Canfield and Mark Hansen, authors of the *Chicken Soup for the Soul* books, do an excellent job of presenting this concept in their new book, *The Aladdin Factor*. Aladdin, as the myth goes, discovered a dusty, dirty, dented lamp. Running his fingers across it, he found an inscription: "Ask and it shall be given." As Aladdin read these words, the lamp shook, and a booming voice sounded, "Who are you, and why have you called me?"

Aladdin was stunned. The genie who emerged from the lamp told Aladdin he would help him obtain all he desired. What did Aladdin want? He wanted people to recognize him, not as a poor beggar, but as a prince. If that happened, Aladdin was certain that all the riches of the kingdom would be his. The genie granted his request, and the transformation transpired.

It is, obviously, folly to believe that a genie will appear from nowhere to make our dreams come true. "Magical thinking" has no place in the plans of God-inspired dreamers. A dream doesn't magically or supernaturally come true just because we want it to. God is not a genie in a magic lamp, and prayer is not a summons for God to do our bidding. It is foolish, for example, to decide that God should provide the funding for a dream by bringing Ed MacMahon to your door with a check for ten million dollars, then sit back and wait for the doorbell to ring.

Too many people, like Aladdin, think all they have to do is *ask* and some magic genie will provide the answers and opportunities. Make a careful analysis and you will see that people considered "lucky" are generally those who—by their actions and attitudes—ask, seek, knock, and then discover opportunities. This requires living by faith.

Canfield and Hansen wrote *The Aladdin Factor* to help others become free to fulfill their dreams. In their book, they reveal five obstacles that keep people from seeing and seizing opportunity: ignorance, erroneous beliefs, fear, pride, and low self-esteem.[9]

Let's consider how a combination of several of those obstacles, including low self-esteem, nearly derailed one woman's dream. Growing up in poverty, Ellen dreamed she'd one day be rich enough to escape the abuse and degradation she watched her mother endure. But after two abusive marriages that left her feeling worthless, and then losing her job, Ellen feared her dream was hopelessly dead.

But, no—Ellen determined to reach out and *do something*. Not simply wait for fate to take a cruel course; not simply wait for a miracle. Responding to a newspaper ad for a support group for women in similar circumstances, Ellen joined Women Empowered. One day, the women wrote down adjectives to describe the others in the group. Ellen was startled to hear herself described as assertive, determined, and friendly. The destructive effects of years of condemnation began to be reversed, and Ellen seized a new—more specific—dream: to hold down a good job that involved working with her hands, the kind of "tinkering" she had always enjoyed.

Ellen enrolled in a trade school, learning about refrigeration and air-conditioning. But she did more than study; her extracurricular activities included chairing a women's group and organizing a school newspaper and a work-study program.

After graduation, Ellen was without work for more than a year. But she kept seeking and knocking and a door opened. She landed a maintenance job with the Chicago Housing Authority, allowing her to achieve her goal of providing for her own livelihood; it also offered the promise of advancement through an apprenticeship program.[10]

Whether planning a dream or trying to recover from a setback, opportunities are everywhere. With God's guidance we must actively ask, seek, and knock to make the most of opportunity.

> With God's guidance we must actively ask, seek, and knock to make the most of opportunity.

God, who is the *God* of our dreams—not the genie—urges us not to sit and wait for serendipity but to seek his advice, obey his instruction, and then get moving.

The dynamic dream equation

$$\text{TALENT} + \text{GOD'S CALL} + \text{PREPARATION} + \text{OPPORTUNITY} =$$
$$\text{WAKING UP YOUR DREAMS}$$

is powerfully effective. The sum total derived from applying these steps all together—waking up your dreams—far exceeds the results of the parts taken in isolation. Eliminating any of these steps greatly diminishes your chances of realizing a great God-inspired and God-enabled dream. I encourage you to apply this equation to your own life and wake up your dream.

It is important for dreamers to be wide awake, particularly when negotiating their dreams' danger zones.

FIVE

ℐℛ

Negotiating Your Dream Danger Zones

ARING TO DREAM BIG dreams is not for the fainthearted. Like alpine skiing, it can be downright dangerous, because the size of your dream, like the steepness of the slope, determines the size of the danger you'll face.

When I arrived in Phoenix in 1978, I began to work toward the fulfillment of my dream. As I lived out each day daring to follow my dreams, I ran into all kinds of detours and dangerous curves. Half of my congregation left. I didn't get paid for weeks at a time because the church couldn't afford to pay me. Often I cried, but *always* I dreamed. My dream was big, and so were the dangers.

Every dreamer faces difficulty. The question is, how can we keep our dreams alive and ourselves committed while traveling through the danger zones?

DREAM CATCHERS

ON A RECENT VISIT to spectacular Sedona, Arizona, I saw a leather-wrapped circle encompassing a web of nylon threads. Streamers decorated with sparkling beads and feathers dangled from the circle. A sign identified the object as a dream catcher.

I learned that these dream catchers have been used by certain Plains Indian tribes for years. These Indians believe that dreams, both good and bad, descend from the dark night skies. Bad dreams are trapped in the web of the dream catcher and evaporate in the early morning sun. Good dreams pass through the center of the web to settle on the person sleeping below.

These dream catchers often hung from babies' cradles; they were carried in ceremonies and celebrations. In their hair, dancers wore miniature dream catchers made of horsehair and chokecherry wood. Today you see dream catchers hanging on walls or dangling from a car's rearview mirror.

Dream catchers illustrate an awareness of dream danger zones. While I am not superstitious, nor do I believe that a dream catcher hanging somewhere will prevent bad things from happening to us, I do believe that our actions and frame of

> *ℐℛ*
>
> **You might call these four words "dream catchers":** *prepare, share, dare,* **and** *care.*

mind can help us filter out—prevent—disaster on the way to the fulfillment of our God-given dreams. You might call these four words "dream catchers": *prepare, share, dare,* and *care.*

In chapter 4, we discussed a few tangible aspects of *preparation* for capturing one's dreams. Here I want to delve deeper into preparation, but mostly I will focus on three things a dreamer needs to do to live out his or her dream: *share, dare,* and *care.* Sharing your dream grounds you in support you'll need to live your dream. *Daring* and *caring* involve critical attitudes and actions needed at every stage of your dream fulfillment.

SHARE

A NUMBER OF PSYCHOLOGICAL studies show that people who seem happiest frequently have strong interpersonal relationships or relational networks providing companionship, a sense of connection, and a sharing of confidences. Happy people often have a faith that includes an interdependent, mutually encouraging and supporting community—giving them a sense of purpose, a focus beyond themselves, self-acceptance, and hope.[1]

Networking is the popular word today for this sort of sharing. Networking reminds me of a child's construction set. Beginning with a single hub from a box of separate rods and connectors, then adding rod by rod, connection by connection, a structure takes shape. It doesn't take many experiments to show a child that the sturdiest structures are those strengthened by connections in several directions. Dreamers need to realize that same truth. We need to connect with others and build a substantial network to shape strong dreams.

My friend Ken got acquainted with George through an introduction by a mutual friend. Today they work together developing a lifetime business dream that both longed to realize.

You increase the chances of realizing your dream tremendously when you share, or network, your dream with others. In doing so, you receive encouragement from many sources, your own commitment to your dream deepens, and you build necessary momentum. Through the sharing process, we also receive wise input from other people, which clarifies and sharpens the dream in our own mind. A proverb states: "As iron sharpens iron, so one [person] sharpens another."[2]

Talking with others about our dream sparks new, and often better, ideas. Writer James Burke's critically acclaimed BBC television production *Connections* traced the evolution of inventions like the computer, going back hundreds of years through the development of such seemingly unrelated things as waterwheels, carillons, the printing press, and the jacquard loom. Down through the ages, inventors and innovators have drawn upon the work of others who came before them or worked alongside them. Dreamers, too, stand on the shoulders of those who've dreamed before or lean on others who are by their side.

Networks Nudge New Dreams

NOT LONG AGO, I was recording some leadership tapes with a publishing company in Nashville. During one of the breaks, I shared with the producer and the engineer a dream I had for teenagers to have performing centers on our soon-to-be-developed two-hundred-acre campus. Since I believe teens need a positive place to discover, grow, play, display their talents, and wake up their dreams, I imagined building a teen "city of dreams."

The producer said I needed to check out contemporary Christian musician Michael W. Smith's Rocketown, because it was a "happening teenage nightclub." That night my son, Patrick, and I went to Rocketown and were very impressed. An incredible band was playing there. We saw state-of-the-art musical production technology, great recreation centers, and an attractive food court. Rocketown's college-age volunteers encouraged and counseled teens who needed someone to talk with.

Michael W. Smith was at the club that evening, so my son and I introduced ourselves to him. I was able to share my dream for teens with him. It was a great networking opportunity. He suggested we work together to build a Rocketown in Arizona on our new campus. My response was an enthusiastic "YES!" Michael said he'd dreamed of franchising the Rocketown idea.

Our conversation gave birth to some new dreams in me: an entire village for teenagers—named Teentown. My dream for teens has grown from the original idea of a performing center to a miniature city with a teen nightclub, a teen cafe, a teen-talk radio station, a recreation facility, a teen leadership center, a media studio, a place for teen counseling, and a teen shelter.

I admit: To be realized and built, this dream will need financial resources. But networking can open doors; as I share the dream with others, interest is growing from major corporations as well as from interested individuals.

Networks Broaden a Dream's Base

ON SIGNING THE DECLARATION of Independence, Benjamin Franklin remarked, "We must all hang together, else we shall all hang separately." The Bible says:

> Though one may be overpowered,
> two can defend themselves.
> A cord of three strands is not quickly broken.[3]

When I first came to Phoenix with a dream, I immediately looked for people to share it with. In doing that, my personal dream became a congregational dream, with thousands of others involved. Then the congregational dream became a community dream, with thousands more participating.

Every week, people from across the country visit and look for help and inspiration from Community Church of Joy, so the community dream has become a national dream.

Finally, the national dream has become an international dream. In November of 1995, I led a seminar with four thousand participants from Europe. Leaders from around the world were interested in learning from our experience at Community Church of Joy.

Throughout this process, I have grown and my dream has grown as well. In a sense, my dream has become our dream. When we built our family life center at Community Church of Joy, all of us were invited to paint our names on one of the concrete blocks. It took thousands of blocks to complete the building, just as it took thousands of people to build the dream.

Networks Accomplish Dreams

IT ALWAYS TAKES TEAMWORK to accomplish great dreamwork. Teresa Filleman knows this well. Eating dinner by the pool at a planning retreat for her church one weekend, Teresa Filleman envisioned a steel drum band as a tool to reach into the church's growing community. She shared her dream with her pastor, who was enthusiastic. The eighty-member congregation was supportive, and together they set about making the dream a reality. As Teresa shared her dream, she built it.

When the first three drums arrived, Teresa relates, "I grabbed my neighbor and said, 'Come on, Sarah, we can do this.' She said, 'Have you ever played them before?' and I said, 'No, but we can figure it out. Some way or other, this is going to work!'" Adding three more members, Teresa's two sons and Sarah's son, the steel drum band "Birds of Steel" took flight.

By playing and continuing to share her dream with others, in three years Teresa has seen the band grow from five to twenty-one members, with drummers ranging from third graders to retirees. Birds of Steel now has an outreach into schools, senior centers, churches, and the community—even across the state—that Teresa says she couldn't have envisioned when she began the group.

One little girl whose mother had just died came to a summer class Teresa and Sarah offered at a neighborhood elementary school. One day, a woman caring for the child came to Sarah after class and said she couldn't believe the difference she saw in the girl. "When she comes home, all she can talk about is the steel drums. She wakes up happy and excited. This is the first thing she's shown interest in since her mother died."

Looking at the impact the band has had, Teresa reflects, "It's had many ramifications I would never have thought of when I said, 'Gee, I've had a vision.'"

Teresa's dream has touched the community and the band members. Dawn Malloy, one of Birds of Steel's newest members, said she'd always wanted to play an instrument. As a child with an interest in music, she struggled learning to play the piano and eventually gave up. She had wanted to play the drums, but had abandoned the dream because her parents had said it wasn't "ladylike."

Coming to the band just a few months before a crisis in her life, Dawn is certain that God led her there. Beyond providing an avenue for Dawn to realize her dreams—playing drums and marching in a Festival of Lights parade—Birds of Steel provided a base of solid friendships, a positive network that supported her through a difficult time of personal struggle. "It's given me a purpose and a way to share my talents with others," says Dawn.

Teresa says, "When I first started the band, I really didn't know where we were going to go with it. I knew it would be fun to do, playing at church every now and then, but I didn't realize, even when I first envisioned it, what the possibilities were."

I offer one more example of how networks can help build dreams. As you build your dream, consider ways in which your dream can help someone else build theirs. This is evidenced in what I call my congregation's "tree story." There were 10,500 citrus trees on the acreage we purchased in 1994. On this land, we plan to build one of the world's largest mission centers, a community with something for everyone: our sanctuary and education complex, of course, but also Teentown, a leadership development center, prayer center, a retirement resort, the Joy Community School, a performing arts and conference center, a memorial garden, a residence quarter, and a chapel.

Someone asked how we were going to afford to remove the trees to begin construction. Even though we didn't have the answer to that question, we moved ahead and purchased the property. We took this risk in faith, which I'll talk about later in the chapter.

Where were we going to get the money to remove the trees—nearly $150,000? In searching for a solution, we learned that a freeway construction company needed to rent some vacant land on which to store some of its heavy equipment. We negotiated a rental agreement with the company: If they removed the trees and graded the land to get it ready to build on, they could use five acres of our land for fifteen months to store their machinery. Our resources complemented theirs, and vice versa.

Networks Keep Dreams on Track

PAT RILEY, THE WELL-KNOWN professional basketball coach, now of the Miami Heat, wrote about what happens when we don't network and look for support and feedback from others. When we don't pair up, he believes we flare up with the chronic "Disease of Me," that I referred to in chapter 3. Pat writes, "A moment in the movie *Wall Street* crystallized for me the biggest reason why teams break down."

Riley goes on to describe a scene from the movie—a large corporate meeting with managers and shareholders, people who should be working for the same goals, but who are arguing for their own personal, selfish interests. A corporate raider seized a microphone and took control of the meeting, saying, "Greed is good." Pat went on to support his point that greed is the primary reason people don't pair up in dreaming. When greed is acceptable, the center of attention becomes "me" and not "we."

"Greed is good," which came to symbolize the dark side of the decade of the eighties, actually is from a real-life speech delivered to a group of students by Ivan Boesky—for a short time considered one of America's most astute businessmen. However, he was convicted of insider trading and later took his turn as being one of the country's most famous federal prisoners.

"That phrase, 'Greed is good,' represented a way of thinking that became rampant," Riley noted. "People were deemed fools unless they grabbed for everything they could get. Little signposts everywhere in the popular culture announced it—slogans declaring how 'You only go around once in life,' slogans asking, 'Who says you can't have it all?' For much of the 1980s, greed defined the tone of the times. We're just beginning to understand fully how much this greed orgy cost us all as a nation, as a team."[4]

Greed produces selfishness, and selfishness produces self-destruction, which leads to dream destruction. To avoid its potential to knock out your "suspension" and steering, share your dream. Pair up in the spotlight as well as in the darkness; share the glory as well as the grief. It's a lot less lonely, a lot more fruitful, and a lot more fun to share your dream.

Networks Prepare Dreamers to Foresee and Avert Obstacles

DANGER IS NO STRANGER to dreamers and their dreams. We shouldn't be surprised or fearful when it comes, but people in our networks—especially trusted dream mates—can help prepare us to see obstacles that might be ahead. My good friend Lyle Schaller warned me about moving our church to a new two-hundred-acre site. He said, "The possibility of failure is greater than the possibility of success. Watch out for thin ice. Just like frozen lakes in the Midwest during winter, the water is not frozen the same thickness everywhere."

Lyle didn't tell me this to scare me; he told me this to prepare me. Knowing that optimistic caution was required helped me not just survive, but thrive.

As we planned and prepared for relocation, we again turned to a network—finding the best people possible to think through and work out all the details of relocation. We created a new company, The Joy Company, tasked with a mission: to take care of the details of planning and zoning, architectural designs, fund raising, and other development issues surrounding the entire relocation process. This company has integrated essential resources and is doing a remarkable job in marketing and public relations.

Trustworthy friends—people who respect you and your dream enough to be honest with you—can also help you "guard your blind side." What do I mean? Let me illustrate: Driving her dad's brand-new car on her eighteenth birthday, my wife, Mary (though she wasn't my wife yet), approached a busy intersection. She stopped at the intersection, looked both ways, and started through the intersection. At that instant, she heard screeching tires, followed by a crunch. A motorcyclist on her right had been traveling in her blind spot; Mary never saw him coming. Fortunately no one was hurt, the only damage being to the car and motorcycle.

All of us have blind spots in our vision—sometimes referred to as the blind side—that make it possible for us to be hit without any warning. One way to keep our dream from being "blindsided" is to double check before moving ahead. Check with God through prayer, and check with a friend you trust. Guarding your blind side can prevent hazardous collisions in our dreams.

Sharing, or networking, our dreams can help strengthen our dreams and keep them on course. But to move ahead in building our dreams we also must dare and care.

DARE AND CARE

THE GREATEST CHALLENGE IN living out a great dream is daring to take the first step. Dare to begin. Dare to jump in!

On January 13, 1982, a jetliner taking off from National Airport struck a bridge separating Washington, D.C., from Virginia, and plunged into the icy Potomac River. A crowd of horrified onlookers gathered on shore, watching and waiting. Suddenly, Lenny Skutnick burst out of the crowd and dove into the ice-choked river to save the life of a drowning woman. Lenny dared to take action. He dared to risk.

His action raised the question: Why did the majority simply stand still and watch? They may have cared about the passenger victims. But, as we'll see care—or passion—must be married to dare—to act, to risk, to overcome fear. Eleanor Roosevelt once told a friend, "You must do the thing you cannot do."

> The greatest challenge in living out a great dream is daring to take the first step. Dare to begin. Dare to jump in!

In his book *Further Along the Road Less Traveled*, M. Scott Peck states,

One of the few things that never ceases to amaze me is how relatively few people understand what courage is. Most people think that courage is the absence of fear. The absence of fear is not courage; the absence of fear is some kind of brain damage. Courage is the capacity to go ahead in spite of the fear, or in spite of the pain.[5]

In the book *Everyone's a Coach*, *care* is referred to as *conviction*.[6] Without conviction or passion, a dreamer will almost certainly get bogged down when the dream seems impossible to reach. Listen to the later compositions of Ludwig von Beethoven and you can hear the depth of *passion* in his music. Beethoven may have made the music, but it's also true that music made Beethoven. Even after he became deaf, the passion to compose drove him to write new and wonderful music that he heard only in his imagination, not with his ears. Despite the pain of deafness, Beethoven dared to risk composing music that his critics would judge when he had not heard it himself.

Great dreams are not cheap; they call for dreamers who dare and care. This may be evident if I introduce another acronym that describes the mindset a dreamer needs to fulfill a dream:

D   Determination
R   Risk
E   Expectation of a good outcome
A   Aspiration
M   Motivation

Determination

CAPTURING ANY DREAM REQUIRES an inordinate amount of determination.

Extraordinary dreams come true when *ordinary* people have an *extraordinary* amount of determination.

As I previously mentioned, I ran the Fiesta Bowl Marathon in 1983. Earlier, I gave you a number of details about my preparation, but I left out a few particulars, especially of the run itself. Some weeks prior to the marathon, I involved my larger network in my dream, asking church members and friends to pledge money for every mile I ran; this would help raise several thousand dollars for our new church facility. The challenge to me came when those who pledged the most said they would pay up only if I finished the entire 26.2 miles of the run. That helped give me the determination I needed to finish the race when a ligament in my ankle tore on the twenty-second mile. In great pain, I hobbled and limped, putting nearly all my weight on one foot for the last 4.2 miles. I determined nothing was going to stop me—*nothing*.

> *Extraordinary dreams come true when ordinary people have an extraordinary amount of determination.*

The engine that drives determination is *commitment*. Dedicated, determined dreamers are not willing to sing "Que sera, sera. Whatever will be, will be." On the night before Mary and I were married, we went for a moonlit walk. As we dreamed about our future together, we made a commitment to each other that to this day underlies our formal wedding vows. We committed: "We will be together for the rest of our lives. No matter what happens, we will stay together. There will be choices to make. We can choose to be happily married, or we can choose to be miserable. It is our decision. Divorce will not be an option. Whatever we need to do to work out problems, we promise to do it."

> **No great dream comes to be unless the dreamer is ready and willing to stay with it when things get tough—which they will.**

This determined pledge has been at the core of what has helped us live out our marital dream. No great dream comes to be without determination. That's because no great dream comes to be unless the dreamer is ready and willing to stay with it when things get tough—which they will.

To my thinking, the bristlecone pine—growing in an arid, inhospitable climate at an elevation of ten thousand feet in the Sierra Nevadas—sets the record for determination. The oldest bristlecone pines discovered (so far) are more than four thousand years old. These trees grow in shallow limestone soil where the average precipitation is not even ten inches a year. They endure scorching heat in the summer, bitter cold in the winter, and high winds that twist them into shapes reminiscent of living driftwood.

Amazingly, bristlecone pines on the harsher south-facing slopes fare better than those on the seemingly more opportune north slopes. Moisture from lingering snows on a north slope increases the prevalence and growth rate of the pine but also fosters organisms that attack the trees. On drier south slopes, bristlecones grow more slowly; their wood becomes highly resinous, which deters both insects and decay. The trees that face an added "obstacle" actually live longer.

While the bristlecone is "determined" naturally, people must choose to be determined. Determination is a choice. Daily we must choose to:

> Press on!
> Nothing in the world
> Can take the place of persistence and determination.
> Talent will not;
> Nothing is more common
> Than unsuccessful people
> With talent.
> Genius will not;
> Unrewarded genius
> Is almost a proverb.
> Education will not;
> The world is full of
> Educated derelicts.
> Persistence and *determination*
> Alone are important."

Author Unknown

Dr. Heidi Hammel, a world-class astronomer, was one of six team leaders who observed, by means of the Hubble Space Telescope, the comet Shoemaker-Levy crashing into Jupiter. What a dream come true! But the voyage to that dream had not come easily. Years earlier as a student, Hammel had felt very out of place taking her first astronomy course at Massachusetts Institute of Technology. She was a sophomore—and a woman—while the rest of the students were seniors or grad students—and male. But the instructor urged Hammel not to quit. Through her own teaching and in speaking engagements across the country, Dr. Hammel, now a principal research scientist at MIT, encourages other young people to pursue their dreams in science.[7]

She overcame obstacles herself, but in a letter to me, Hammel wrote,

> If you want to talk about having dreams and pursuing them, then the person you should really talk to is my mother, Phyllis Hammel. As a young woman, she had a dream of being a pastor, but women didn't do that. So she became a nurse, got married, and had kids. After she finished raising three children (while also working full-time as a psychiatric nurse), she went to college at nights to get a bachelors degree. Then she retired from the hospital, packed up her home of over 20 years in Pennsylvania, and moved across the country to enroll in a theological seminary in Chicago. She is now well into her second year of leading a congregation (back in Pennsylvania), and she loves it. Now *that* is a woman who had a dream, and did whatever it took to attain it!

When you dream a great dream, don't play it safe; take a risk. Think about Columbus setting out to explore the outer edges of his dream—beyond the edge of any map. When he and his crew "sailed off the map," they had to chart a completely new course. Had Columbus decided to play it safe and turn back, he would never have experienced the dream of his life.

There are two ways for you to "get behind your dreams" in terms of backing them up, of being the one responsible for them. One is a good and responsible route to take: backing them up, giving them your best. But there's another way of looking at the term that leads to disaster: If we always opt for what is cautiously comfortable, we will find ourselves getting *behind* our dreams, holding back or lagging behind or even hiding behind them rather than being out in front of them, leading the way. Beware when responsible caution turns into a continual caution whose aim is not the preservation of the dream, but of the dreamer's comfort zone. That kind of caution rapidly turns into procrastination, a dead end for any dream.

People who wait for all the lights to turn green before they take a trip never leave home. The obstacle of fear has blocked countless great dreams. In the advice of David Lloyd George, "Don't be afraid to take a big step if one is indicated. You can't cross a chasm in two small jumps."8

Though fear may make us feel inclined to take small steps, faith can galvanize us to take the leap that gets us safely across the chasm. The essence of faith is risk, not caution. Faith *makes* things happen, while caution simply *watches* things happen.

> The essence of faith is risk, not caution. Faith *makes* things happen, while caution simply *watches* things happen.

Fear is really the opposite of faith; it is impossible to hold a fear thought and a faith thought in your mind at the same time. I encourage you to choose the faith thought. As the mother said to her three-year-old upon his first encounter with a bubble gum machine, "You have to give up the nickel to get the gum." You can't hang on to fear and walk in faith. Where there is faith-thinking, there is risk-taking.

You might expect people to be fearful of handling babies born to HIV-positive mothers. Too many people *are* afraid, especially in Nairobi, Kenya, where the World Health Organization predicts that by the end of this year there will be three thousand children who were born HIV positive. These babies are regularly abandoned by their families, condemned to die of starvation and neglect on the streets. The real tragedy is that three out of four children born HIV positive will test negative within eighteen months and could live out a healthy life.

Realizing there were no facilities existing to rescue and care for these children, Father Angelo D'Agostino, an American physician-priest working in Africa, envisioned a place where these abandoned or orphaned children could live and run and find a loving, homelike atmosphere, a place where those who developed full-blown AIDS could live—and die—with dignity and surrounded by love. His efforts, and those of others who caught the power of his vision, led to the founding of Nyumbani (Swahili for "home") on September 8, 1992.

Because fear is not a factor for Father D'Agostino and those who share his dream, sixty youngsters have been given a home; only four have died.

"The kids are running and cheerful and healthy," Father D'Agostino says. "Most would have died in four or five months of neglect if they didn't come here." Father D'Agostino and his associates had the courage to dream a God-sized dream.

The Bible tells us how to handle fear:

The Lord is my light and my salvation—whom shall I fear?[9]

For God did not give us a spirit of timidity, but a spirit of power, of love, and of self-discipline.[10]

I encourage you to unlock the courage that God placed at the heart of your dream.[11]

Expectation of a Good Outcome

OUR POSITIVE EXPECTATIONS at the beginning of every endeavor will immeasurably impact the final outcome of our dreams. Vince Lombardi, the former coach of the world-champion Green Bay Packers, told his players at the beginning of every football game, "We can only win if we *expect* to win."

Not expecting our dreams to come true is like a loud noise on a snowy slope: It starts an avalanche. It's like the first mishap of a ten-car pileup on the freeway. There's a "snowballing" effect to low expectations. I expect they cause more dream fatalities than any other dream killer.

When I was a kid, our high school track coach taught us that hurdlers must run as though they *expect* to clear the hurdles—or they never will. A hurdler who fears catching a foot on the hurdle will either pull up short of the hurdle, crash into it, or run too slowly to win a race.

The principle works the same for dreamers. Let's examine these *positive* and *negative* expectations. Negative expectations are

Low expectations, which cause the dreamer to be fearful.
No expectations, which cause the dreamer to be doubtful.
Slow expectations, which cause the dreamer to be too careful.

Positive expectations are

Go expectations, which inspire both dream and dreamer.
Grow expectations, which give roots to both dream and dreamer.
Glow expectations, which give joy to both dream and dreamer.

A friend recently told me that a childhood experience had changed her perspective on expectations. It only took one hike, chancing upon berry bushes and arriving home with purple pockets and crushed berries, to convince her that she should always carry an empty container of some kind. Zip-closed plastic bags and empty film canisters are standard-issue gear in her family on any outing.

"Now, because we go prepared—expecting to find something wonderful—my kids have water from the Pacific, sand from the Colorado River, delicate hummingbird nests, porcupine quills, dazzling quartz crystals, tiny pine cones, and iridescent bird feathers—things they can always treasure because we were prepared to find them." Expect the best from your dreams. Think of it as carrying a zip-closed bag!

Expecting a good outcome can bolster the courage you need to take risks. Shankill Road, on the "peace line" dividing the Catholic and Protestant sections of Belfast, Northern Ireland, is not a place of security. Yet there a young man named Jackie has established a community street outreach center. Tom Eggum, Community Church of Joy's director of mission and outreach, met Jackie on a 1994 trip to Ireland. Jackie took Tom to visit the Shankill Road center and introduced Tom to his co-workers, who share the love of Christ in this battered neighborhood. More than a few of them have been assigned to this ministry upon their release from prison. Many have themselves been part of the violence on both sides.

A young man who had attempted to kill Jackie was about to come before a judge for sentencing. Incredibly, this young man asked Jackie to write a positive statement to present to the judge, and Jackie's letter helped shorten the man's prison sentence. Jackie shared with Tom how much he looked forward to sharing his faith with this young man, as the judge had given him a community service assignment at Jackie's mission after his release from prison. For Jackie, the expectation of a good outcome turned a risk into an opportunity.

Aspiration

TO ASPIRE MEANS TO set our sights on the highest goals and objectives life has to offer. If you turn the root word to an adjective—*aspiring*—its synonyms are *eager*, *enthusiastic*, *impassioned*, and *soaring*.

To aspire to any goal, one must have hope. Psychologist C. R. Snyder of the University of Kansas cited the importance of hope as a predictor of academic achievement for first-semester freshman university students. Think about his findings: "Students with high hope set themselves higher goals and know how to work hard to attain them. When you compare students of equivalent intellectual aptitude on their academic achievements, what sets them apart is hope."[12]

Hope, as defined by Snyder, is not blind, unfounded optimism, but the belief that you have the will and the capacity to achieve your goals. Using a scale developed to objectively assess how much hope a person has, Dr. Snyder has found that people with "high hope" tend to be more successful and better able to handle difficult times.

People with high hopes are people who look ahead into the future and are confident that they can soar—as they choose to or are forced to "leave the nest." Here's what I mean:

I learned a great deal about soaring by reading about how eagles learn to fly. When the little eaglets are born, they are surrounded by a soft, comfortable nest. As they grow, their daily nourishment is provided for them. At first, all they have to do is open their mouths and receive the food their parents drop in.

When the mother senses that it is time for the eaglets to learn to soar, she removes some of the comfortable padding that lines the nest. She then nudges the eaglets to the edge and pushes them over the side, swooping down to catch them on her strong wings. It would be more comfortable for the eaglets to keep being fed and resting in the fluffy nest. But they were born to fly. With that hope in mind (if birds can hope), they take flight.

If you haven't already done so, I challenge you to write down your goals and objectives and inscribe them deeply on the tablet of your heart and mind. Fixing our aspirations firmly in our minds and hearts helps us rise above obstacles that present themselves and, with our eyes focused clearly on our goal, fly steadily toward fulfillment of our dreams.

Henry David Thoreau said: "If one advances confidently in the direction of their dreams, and endeavors to live the life they have imagined, they will meet with a success unexpected in an uncommon hour."

Advancing confidently and enthusiastically in the direction of our dreams is the only way dreamers can be ready to soar.

Motivation

MOTIVATION ORIGINATES IN THE inner chambers of the dreamer's heart. External influences can be informative and insightful, but not necessarily motivational. Our values, purposes, and convictions develop our motivation. As you work toward and hone your dream, periodically stop and give yourself a "motivation check." Ask yourself:

1. Will my dream heal or hurt?
2. Will my dream fill a need?
3. Will my dream solve a problem?
4. Will my dream help others' dreams come true?

If you answered "no" to any of the four, go back and reexamine your dream.

After arriving in Phoenix, I met once a week—every Friday—with a local high school football team. My role was to provide motivational inspiration. The team's spirit was in the pits; it was a new school, and after several seasons they hadn't won a game. My deepest desire was to help each player develop the motivation of a champion. Many of the young men did develop winning motivation. One of them was Art Caswell, who had a dream to become a professional football player with the Raiders. He doggedly pursued the dream until he was twenty-six, when he made the team! It's rare for any rookie to be that old. He'd played awhile with the Canadian Football League. He was cut, but that setback only made his motivation grow. Then he played semi-pro without pay, unloading trucks during the day and practicing football at night. Friends would say, "Give it up," but Art kept chasing his dream. He could persist because he was motivated within to do the most he possibly could with his God-given ability.

This kind of determination was motivated at a deep, personal level. The obstacles he faced taught Art humility, patience, sacrifice, and compassion. In someone else, the same setbacks might have produced envy, bitterness, impatience, and hardness of heart. What made the difference for Art? Art knew that the greatest coach imaginable believed in him and his dream.

Knowing God cared for and believed in him helped Art forge solid qualities of character, which are the basis for a solid motivation. When the dreamer's motivation is right, the dream is right, and the dreamer wins. So does everyone else!

When a dreamer's motivation is wrong, there is little lasting sense of fulfillment in accomplishing the dream. After twelve years of a "dream come true" playing baseball in the major leagues, Bernie Carbo still felt empty and unfulfilled. Bernie may be best known for hitting the home run for the Boston Red Sox that gave them a tie in the sixth game of the 1975 World Series. But at the height of his dream, Bernie despised himself. He'd wasted those "dream come true" years in abusing drugs and alcohol. He was alienated from his parents. He didn't even think his life was worth living.

Through the help of a teammate, Bernie checked into a rehabilitation center. There he met a man, a retired minister, who shared with him that God had a better purpose for Bernie's life; God could help him find freedom from his captivity to drugs and alcohol. That was nearly twenty years ago, and Bernie still calls on God every morning to help him walk in his freedom. Today Bernie helps youngsters learn the basics of baseball and the source of true motivation in Diamond Club, a baseball school he began near Tampa, Florida.[13]

Positive, productive motivation propels a dreamer to overcome the roughest obstacles.

The Dare-Care Duo

THE FIVE DARE-CARE ELEMENTS work together to give a dreamer the strength to see a dream through to its fulfillment.

D   Determination
R   Risk
E   Expecting a good outcome
A   Aspiration
M   Motivation

My friends Barbie and Eric Swanson have lived out the dare-care duo for the past sixteen years. Barbie and Eric dreamed, in vain, of having children. One day, their doctor told them of a three-day-old baby boy available for adoption. This was their dream come true! But in time their new son, Christopher, was diagnosed as having pervasive developmental disorders.

This troubling discovery only strengthened Barbie and Eric's commitment to their son. Throughout the sixteen years that they have helped Christopher along, they have always—*always*—cared more about what is *best* for Christopher than about what is easiest for them.

Every great dreamer dares enough to do, and cares enough to be, what is *best*, not what's *easiest*. People have frequently asked Barbie and Eric, "Are you going to keep Christopher?" That's ridiculous! Christopher is their son. They care about him and his future.

If we really care about our dreams, we must not be haphazard, leaving the fulfillment of our dreams to chance. Haphazardness is hazardous to your dream's health. A synonym for *haphazard* is *careless*. If our dreams originate in the mind of God, and God passes them on to us, we had better care what happens to them. Our dream may be a dream that God will use to change a life or even to change the world. I encourage you to love your dream, and the dreamer within yourself, as much as God does. Develop passion for your dream.

Let God be the God of your dreams. Then sharing, daring, and caring passionately about your dreams will take you far along the road to a fantastic future.

Successfully negotiating our dreams' danger zones isn't easy, but it is essential if we are to see our dreams fulfilled. Dr. Robert Schuller, in his book *Power Thoughts for Power Living*, provides helpful insight for every dreamer. He writes:

> Build a dream and the dream builds you.
> Most people don't know this. It's true.
> Build a dream and the dream builds you.

Dr. Schuller tells about Walt Disney's dream to make feature-length animated motion pictures. In the 1930s, no one had ever considered such a thing before, but Disney began work on *Snow White and the Seven Dwarfs*.

In the end, Disney spent millions to hire over a thousand animators to produce *Snow White and the Seven Dwarfs*, more than other studios had invested in *Gone With the Wind* and *The Wizard of Oz* combined. In the years following the Depression, it was unthinkable to spend so much on an animated movie.

> Every great dreamer dares enough to do, and cares enough to be, what is *best*, not what's *easiest*.

When the equipment or techniques to do what he wanted didn't exist, Disney's people invented them. When he was down to his last dime, Disney borrowed from every source he could find. Meeting one dream danger zone after another, Walt Disney didn't let anything stand in the way of his dream. "He knew he was on to something," writes Dr. Schuller. In 1937, four years after Disney began work on *Snow White*, the movie opened to critical acclaim and went on to become one of Disney's most beloved films.

The success of *Snow White* laid the foundation for all his succeeding films, for *The Mickey Mouse Club*—which became a television institution—for Disneyland and Disney World, and for all that was and is yet to come from the legacy of Walt Disney. "That was his dream," Dr. Schuller concludes. "Look what it built for him when he built the dream." Then Dr. Schuller asks, "What's your dream? Don't be afraid to start building it. Start right now. Do something to get your dream going today."[14]

Put the foundation down. Lay the cornerstone. The sooner you do, the sooner your dream will build you. Face every dream danger with confidence and courage. When you look back on the dream you framed and fashioned, more amazing than its final edifice may be the new design created within you.

Six

Renewing the Dreamer and the Dream

ONE OF THE MOST memorable events of the decade of the sixties began as twilight faded into night on November 9, 1965. In the Sir Adam Beck power station at Niagara Falls, a tiny arm moved closer and closer to a contact point inside a backup electric power relay, part of a system designed to protect the generators from damage caused by a sudden change of speed. Two years earlier, it had been set to trip at a specific "critical rise" in electric demand flowing northward from the power station. Though power demand had risen in those two years, no one thought to change the relay to deal with the changed reality. At eleven seconds past 5:16 P.M. that day, when power on a transmission line from the Beck station to Toronto briefly rose above 375 megawatts, "the two tiny metal projections made contact, and in doing so set in motion a sequence of events that would lead, within twelve minutes, to chaos."[1]

A signal took the overloaded transmission line out of the system, transferring its load to the other four northbound lines. They immediately tripped out from the overload, and so it went, like a line of dominoes, system by system, until virtually all of the northeast, from New Jersey to Canada, was without electric power. In New York City, roughly 800,000 people were stuck when the subways lost power; hospitals, airports, elevators, traffic signals, utilities, water supplies, and communications were paralyzed. For thirteen hours, normal life came to a standstill, stopped as dead as the circuits.

101

All this occurred because one small, but significant, element of the system went "unrenewed." If dreamers don't constantly monitor and renew themselves, they and their dreams can suffer a similar "blackout." Our dreams can falter—"brownout"—or fail entirely if we don't check our dreams' "power systems" for problems. How can a dreamer and a dream be repaired, renewed, and reenergized? Keep reading.

If your dream is flickering, it's time to inspect your dream circuits. A few lines in a do-it-yourself manual succinctly outline the problem: If your lights go out, or a fuse blows, or a circuit breaker trips, then something needs to be corrected. It makes no sense to replace the fuse or reset the circuit breaker until you have found and corrected the trouble, or you'll blow another fuse or trip the breaker again.

For simple home repairs, the guide suggests checking for four common causes: worn insulation causing bare electric wires to touch, faulty connections, an overloaded motor, or too many appliances on the same circuit.

Let's take that image and apply it to dreamers and dreams. How do you keep the dream circuits working—flowing with spirited and creative energy?

REPLACE THE WORN INSULATION

AT A RECENT BREAKFAST with Larry Jilian, a dynamic business consultant, I learned some secrets that many key CEOs use to keep on dreaming great dreams. When Larry begins a seminar or consultation, he asks that the participants write down all their problematic issues. Then Larry collects the papers in a box and literally kicks the box out of the room. Now that participants have eliminated the negatives, he announces, it's time to get on with developing and living out the dream.

This practical illustration is not meant to indicate that writing our problems on a piece of paper, placing them in a box, and kicking it out of the room will make our problems disappear. That action doesn't *solve* anything, but it does dramatically illustrate the need to recognize and do something about the negatives that shut down our ability to dream.

Character grounded in God's standards of integrity, responsibility, generosity, perseverance, forgiveness, and the like, protect our dreams from shorting or blowing out. Attitude is like insulation around a wire: A sound, positive attitude helps keep the "dream current" flowing steadily and in the right direction. Permit a poor, negative attitude—like a break in the insulation—to surround your life, and watch the sparks fly and the lights go out of your dream! If we're going to replace wires that have broken insulation, first we need to know what "broken insulation" looks like.

> *Character grounded in God's standards of integrity, responsibility, generosity, perseverance, forgiveness, and the like, protect our dreams from shorting or blowing out.*

Let me list a number of thoughts, attitudes, and character traits that will shut down a dream and a dreamer:

Character Traits	Thoughts and Attitudes
Greed	Indifference
Laziness	Worry
Dishonesty	Jealousy
Deception	Resentment
Obsessions	Bitterness
Cheating	Fear
Unforgiveness	Hatred
Addictions	Prejudice
Blaming	Atheism

Cracks in Character

NO ONE IS PERFECT. I'm not asking you to be, nor claiming that I am. But character counts more than credentials, and people are watching. Our basic character affects our dream—our motivations, our methods, and our results. Several years ago, I was nearly bowled over with a new awareness of how *much* our character counts. One summer, our family was preparing for a vacation to Huntington Beach, California. I took the car to be washed, and in the waiting area at the car wash I noticed audiotapes for sale. I picked up two Beach Boys tapes and took them to the cashier. Outside, after paying the cashier, I realized I'd been undercharged. I went back, got in line again, and, when I made it back up to the cashier, said, "I came back to pay you what I owe you. You undercharged me."

Without hesitating, the cashier blurted out, "I know, Reverend. I was in your church last Sunday, and I just wanted to see if you were an honest man."

Wham! I certainly wasn't expecting that response! She was doing a spiritual check to be sure my walk matched my talk. She didn't want to "plug in to" Joy's dream if its "outlet" wasn't "grounded" in integrity. The character of the dreamer affects the course of the dream.

My friend Wayne is a great example of a dreamer with sound character. Wayne spent seven years building his dream, developing one of the most prestigious communities in Texas. When Texas suffered a severe economic downturn in the 1980s, Wayne squarely faced hurdles that other developers around him chose to go under, instead of over. Instead of filing bankruptcy, Wayne chose to make sacrifices, successfully settling the complex issues he faced with his creditors. Today financial institutions esteem Wayne's courage and character highly and frequently consult him.

The other day over lunch, Wayne smiled when he told me it wouldn't have been any "fun" to file bankruptcy. He wouldn't have built a reputation for courage and honesty, either. I realize that sometimes there is no choice about filing for bankruptcy, but if there is a choice, remember that the toughest road can also be the highest.

Cracks in Thoughts and Attitudes

ATTITUDES ARE SHAPED BY thoughts. If our thoughts are negative, impure, and disordered, our attitudes will be, too. Zig Ziglar warns about "stinkin' thinkin'." Stinkin' thinkin' produces stinkin' attitudes, which produce stinkin' dreamin'.

On my thirtieth birthday my "thinkin'" was so "stinkin'" that I couldn't even eat my favorite meal, lovingly prepared by my family. I felt that a man in my congregation had been unfair and unkind to me. He opposed most of the dreams I proposed. I was supposed to meet with him after dinner that night. Anger swelled in me as I rehearsed in my mind how I was going to tell him off. My stomach was so churned and filled with anger that I had no appetite.

When he and I met later that night, the discussion turned into a shouting match. Afterward, I felt embarrassed, humiliated, and devastated. I was in no condition to do anything constructive, let alone dream. After a sleepless night, I went to this man the next day to ask his forgiveness for my negative actions and attitudes. I realized that was the only way I could possibly get beyond myself to dream great dreams. The moment I asked for his forgiveness, I felt the ten-ton weight I'd been carrying removed from my shoulders. I felt free to dream again.

"Cracked insulation"—Zig Ziglar's "stinkin' thinkin'"—in our thoughts and attitudes is usually as apparent to others as is the telltale smell of an electrical device with a problem. The Bible tells us how to take care of the cracks in our thoughts and attitudes: "Let us throw off everything that hinders and the sin that so easily entangles."[2]

New Insulation

IT'S NOT GOOD ENOUGH to simply get rid of old insulation, leaving bare wires. Insulation is an integral part of the total cord or cable package. There are good insulators and poor insulators. In fact, part of the job of a friend of mine is testing different materials in which wires and cables are wrapped for their resistance to crushing, stretching, heat, and chemicals.

❦ Just as insulation is an integral part of a cord or cable, attitude—or mind-set—is an integral part of dreaming. In life, it's important that wires are wrapped in material that will stand up under everyday stresses. It's equally important that dreamers are "wrapped" in the things that will help them keep their positive thoughts and attitudes flowing, even under stress. Dreamers need to replace "faulty insulation"—attitudes and thoughts that are doubtful or negative—wrapping themselves and their dreams instead in hopeful, positive attitudes and thoughts, keeping the power flowing that will help fulfill their dreams.

> ❦
>
> **Wisdom, knowledge and understanding help shield dreamers when problems and negative attitudes threaten to emotionally short-circuit them and their dreams.**

Knowledge, wisdom, and understanding make durable insulation.

Knowledge gives us the facts, wisdom gives us good judgment and common sense, and understanding helps us put them both together into attitudes and actions. All three are essential if we are to realize our dreams.

A great ancient king named Solomon was chosen to be the ruler over a multitude of people. God offered to give Solomon anything he asked for. Solomon could have chosen wealth, honor, or the death of his enemies, but he did not. Without hesitation, Solomon asked for wisdom and knowledge. God responded by telling Solomon that he had chosen well. Solomon's choice led to the fulfillment of every dream he ever had, and everyone came seeking his great counsel. What happened to Solomon can happen to you and me as well. When we choose knowledge, wisdom, and understanding, we too can experience fulfillment.

Applying wisdom, knowledge, and understanding, like insulation, helps shield dreamers when problems and negative attitudes threaten to emotionally short-circuit both dreamers and dreams. Knowing the real facts and exercising common sense, combined with discernment to know how to act on the facts, keeps productive, positive energy flowing through dreamers and their dreams. Just as God enthusiastically gave Solomon wisdom and knowledge when Solomon asked for it, so, too, will God give you wisdom and knowledge if you ask for them.

Responsibility, respect, and *reverence* make excellent insulation. When they hear the word "dreamer," people sometimes have a negative image. This idea probably stems from encounters with irresponsible dreamers. When dreamers jump from one dream to another, never finishing what they have begun, they are irresponsible. When dreamers make exaggerated promises and break them, they are acting unreliably. This responsibility deficit calls into question a dreamer's credibility. Responsible dreamers not only make commitments—they keep them. Every dreamer needs to wrap himself or herself in responsibility.

Respect shouldn't be accorded to dreamers on the basis of their high position or profile. Respect is due dreamers who value others, who treasure and dignify humankind. Jesus Christ respected every individual so much that he gave his life to secure a magnificent future for each of us. True respect values with no trace of exploitation. The dreamers who should be respected are those who are most *respectful*. Both giving and receiving respect helps dreamers to reach their full potential. Respect in both directions insulates the dream and the dreamer.

Great dreamers also need to wrap themselves in reverence. Reverence goes beyond respect to include a sense of heartfelt devotion to God. Reverence cultivates humility and helps dreamers establish a sound sense of their own worth so that when great dreams do come true, dreamers are willing to share the credit, acknowledgment, or applause with God as well as with those who have helped them. Sincere humility helps insulate dreamers from arrogance and helps increase their hearts' capacity to contain compassion and all these other positive attitudes. A big heart is of far more value than a big head.

Replacing bad insulation is not a one-time event. Dreamers need to daily "check their wiring," replacing poor attitudes and thoughts with sound attitudes and thoughts.

CHECK YOUR CONNECTIONS

WHEN AN APPLIANCE WON'T work or when a fuse blows, a second simple thing to check for is a faulty plug—a faulty connection to the power outlet. Dreamers need to ensure they're connected to the power outlet, too. The Bible is a sound "plug" to connect us to God, who is the one true source of the power we need to live out our dreams. In the Bible, Paul advised the Philippians to act on a strategy for positive, power-filled thinking:

> ". . . whatever is true, whatever is noble, whatever is right, whatever is pure, whatever is lovely, whatever is admirable— if anything is excellent or praiseworthy—think about such things."[3]

Remind yourself daily to choose to believe what is true, noble, right, and praiseworthy about yourself, your dream, and others, too—particularly anyone criticizing you. This prevents short circuits of bitterness within you. It may help if you imagine "trashing" the untrue, ignoble, wrong, impure, ugly, and disrespectful attitudes, just as you'd discard bad insulation, wrapping yourself in wisdom and understanding, then plugging in to the power of the noble, the right, the excellent. Repeated practice in choosing to focus on the pure and true makes it easier to recognize and get rid of the negatives before they blow a fuse and cut the power to your dreams.

REPAIR THE DAMAGED MOTOR

WE'VE COMPARED PROBLEMS IN wiring to concerns of our spiritual and emotional well-being. The other two problems that can cut our dream's power have to do with things that disrupt the flow of creative energy and productivity. An electric motor can seize up, or freeze. When it stops turning, a force known as counter electromotive force, which helps control the current, decreases. The increased current coming into the motor will actually burn it out.

There are forces that can "seize up" both dreamer and dream, nonproductive channels that freeze creativity and productivity and increase resistance in the dreamer. The damage these forces may do can burn out a dream. Let's look at five forces that freeze up a dreamer's creativity and increase resistance to living the dream:

Routine
Comfort
Criticism
Weariness
Loneliness

Routine

WHEN WE ARE PUSHED or stressed, we look for the known, the tried, and the familiar. A man recently remarked to me, "People think they know what they like, but in reality they like what they know." The familiar often seems like a *short-cut*, but in the end it may *cut short* your dream. Perhaps we become convinced that routine is best because we know the value of positive routines of daily hygiene, prayer, exercise, study, relationship building, work, and nutrition.

But routine can freeze our creative resources and halt our productivity in the direction of our dream.

> The familiar often seems like a *shortcut*, but in the end it may *cut short* your dream.

Shopping in the same places, eating in the same restaurants, driving the same roads, hanging around the same people, traveling to the same places, saying the same things in the same way, and thinking the same thoughts begin to freeze our creativity and drive.

Routine leaves its impression day by day until at last we find ourselves in a rut. I've heard it said that the only difference between a rut and a grave is the dimensions. And anyone who has ever set up a portable toddler's swimming pool in the lawn knows what you find underneath if you don't frequently move it: dead grass. Tires that are never rotated wear out, unevenly, before their time. Life is filled with examples of the danger of routine.

A friend's family occasionally takes a breather from the grind of the daily routine; the parents declare a "no have-to's day." Many of the family's discretionary rules do not have to be followed for that day. It may mean family members can stay in their pajamas all day; eat ice cream before lunch; sing—loudly—and dance in the house along with the radio; walk barefoot through mud. Within reason, the daily "have-to's" are set aside.

> ✐
>
> **Mistakes can be a highly effective teaching tool to point us toward what we yet need to learn, understand, or practice.**

It helps the family, children included, to make conscious choices to break out of the routine and experience the new, to refresh and take time to enjoy life and each other's company. It helps them see that even the "have to's" are conscious choices. "It helps our children see that those wants that seem so attractive aren't things they'd really want to do *all* the time, and it helps us all to see the routine as something we choose for a reason, not something that chooses for us," the mother says.

Another way to break routine is to daydream. We are frequently more open to creative insights in moments of reverie, when we are "tuned out." The painter Grant Wood recommended that, to get out of a rut, people should try milking a cow. He admitted that some of his most imaginative ideas emerged while he sat beside a cow.

Sometimes people choose to follow the routine in order to avoid making mistakes. *That,* in itself, is a mistake because mistakes can be a highly effective teaching tool to point us toward what we need to learn, understand, or practice. At the Crystal Cathedral recently, I heard Bruce Larson say, "If something is worth doing, it is worth doing poorly." What he meant was not that you should set out to do something poorly, but that you should set out to *do*. If you see or think of something you believe will be really worthwhile, go for it. Break out of your routine and dare to make a mistake. You can learn and improve things along the way, but first you must get moving.

Back to our electric motor analogy: Breaking out of routine occasionally helps us keep our motors running with creativity and productive action. Looking for fresh approaches lessens the "freeze-up" potential of routine. Try asking new questions; questions facilitate creativity. The following list may help you generate questions:

What are other uses for this resource or concept?
What changes could I make to improve this?
How could I combine this with something else?
What would happen if I rearranged elements?
What would happen if I tried the opposite approach?

Break a routine today. Drive an alternate route to work. Try a new recipe. Order from the vegetarian side of the menu. Break a routine and you will meet new people, see new things, or experience a new adventure. Take a new road, sing a new song, make a new friend, act on a new idea. Keep your motor running!

Comfort

COMFORT IS ANOTHER FREEZING force for a dreamer and a dream. We talked about the obstacle of comfort in chapter 5, where we talked about its opposite: risk. But I can't overemphasize its dangers. The lure of comfort lulls dreamers into the easiest, most convenient way to live. A potentially powerful dream has the opposite potential—to call us away from our comfort zone to new horizons.

Jack Hayford tells the tale of a caterpillar that never experienced the thrill of soaring as a butterfly. Jack noticed a caterpillar on the driveway when he went out to get his paper early one morning. Not giving it much thought, he returned to the house, read the paper, and went about his day.

When he retrieved the next morning's paper, he saw the same caterpillar in the same spot. Curious, he examined the potential butterfly and discovered it was dead.

Sadly and gently picking up the creature, he contemplated the cause of its death. Had the caterpillar crawled onto the warm driveway in the cool of the night, only to be baked by the warm California sun gradually sizzling the driveway? What the caterpillar first *perceived* as comfort turned deadly when he didn't keep moving out of his comfort zone.

Realizing one's dreams can be costly—not necessarily in terms of money, but nearly always in physical and emotional terms. In 1776, Thomas Paine, patriot of the American Revolution, wrote about the high cost of the dream of freedom: "What we obtain too cheaply, we esteem too lightly."

After a speaking engagement in Philadelphia last summer, my wife and I visited some of the city's historic sites. What amazed me was the willingness of so many women and men to give up the comforts of life to fight for freedom. We value those who pay a high price for important dreams.

The pursuit of comfort does not build virtues like integrity, responsibility, compassion, and courage. Once we've experienced comfort, its lure can "seize up" our drive. The challenge we face is to put aside comfort for something greater and more motivating—commitment. Commitment is what it takes to make impossible dreams possible.

A few years ago, a woman stood outside our church, too uncomfortable to come in. A friend saw her and invited her into the church. Once she came in, she was surprised by how much she enjoyed the service. This one step out of her comfort zone led her to fulfill spiritual dreams she had had from the time she was a little girl.

Never let comfort seize up your drive. Always remember: God is more interested in our character—and the character of our dreams—than in our comfort.

Criticism

CRITICISM CAN STOP OUR motor cold, especially when we are short on spiritual and emotional energy. Resistance builds quickly, and our wiring fries.

Think of it this way: Superstars are in trouble when they believe everything written about them; likewise, dreamers are in trouble when they begin to believe every criticism leveled at them. Managed improperly, criticism can cripple and even kill a dream and destroy the dreamer. A mature dreamer understands that no one is free of critics. For every positive encourager, there is at least one negative discourager. That's life.

We can let the doubts that criticism engenders stop us in our tracks. Doubt erodes confidence; without confidence, dreamers and their dreams seize up. They wait for someone more capable to take up the dream. They burn out from the heat that builds up when incoming criticism isn't offset by the truth of positive action.

The best advice I've heard for managing criticism involves three simple steps.

First, if the criticism is true, do something about it. Admit and correct your mistake, adjust your attitude, reevaluate your position, and apologize if necessary.

Second, if the criticism is an exaggeration or only partly true, deal with the truth and ignore the rest. Admit and begin to do something to correct the fault, change the focus, make restitution—whatever the true part of the criticism involves.

Third, if the criticism is false or unwarranted, rise above it and go on.

I arrived at Community Church of Joy energetic, enthusiastic, and eager to live out my dream, which called for change—*not* changing the truth, but changing the religious methods and styles that made many people feel church was boring and irrelevant. I quickly encountered resistance, however, to every idea or imaginative thought that introduced change.

The change that new ministry ideas introduced was so challenging to church board members that some "went underground."

They held private meetings to discuss how to get rid of me. They rallied other members to oppose any change that threatened the familiar, comfortable status quo. It was an emotionally charged issue for many of them—and for me.

Finally a congregational meeting was organized to discuss the changes—my first congregational meeting as an ordained pastor. The meeting lasted four hours, with clearly more heat than light exchanged. Many members attacked me verbally and criticized most of my new ideas. It was an excruciatingly painful experience, and I left the meeting so traumatized that I actually became sick when I got home. My body lived out the anguish in my mind and heart.

I cried and prayed, and I made the decision not to let all the criticism and negativity melt my dream.

But nine months of criticism began to take a toll on me. One particularly difficult night, I got into my car and all I could do was cry. At that low point in my life, I felt like such a failure. My dream for the church seemed to be burning out. I prayed: If God wanted me to get out of town or out of the ministry, I'd do it. My heart was aching as my dream seemed to be breaking. Criticism ground me to a halt and nearly burned me out.

At the darkest moment, I sensed God's encouraging embrace freeing me up again. God was stronger than the criticism. He was able to take the pain and turn it into progress. He used the criticism for his purposes, to nudge changes in me. One of these changes was in my attitude. My decision was not to "get even," but to get *going* and *growing*. Criticism didn't destroy the dream; it launched the dream.

When facing criticism, remember that life isn't always fair. Robert Schuller wrote a best-seller with a great title: *Life Is Not Fair ... But God Is Good*. You can hang onto your dreams in the face of anything that is unjust, partial, or unwarranted by remembering that God is good, and that "in all things God works for the good of those who love him, who have been called according to his purpose."[4] Dreamers who let unfair people or circumstances immobilize them can end up abandoning their dreams even moments before they would have been fulfilled.

A thousand things can go well today, yet if I make one mistake—or hear one bit of criticism—that's all I often remember. Because criticism naturally hurts and tends to slow us down, we need to learn that God always has the last word, and it is good!

Weariness

WEARINESS, LIKE TOO GREAT a load, tends to slow our motor down, but the demands on us don't necessarily diminish. Incessant activity, interruptions, deadlines, and the daily moment-to-moment grind all increase our "load." The balance between our strength (our "counter electromotive force") and the demands on us (our load) is lost. We lose our hope, motivation, and spark; in effect, we burn out.

Weariness impairs a dreamer's judgment the way twenty-four hours of nonstop driving impairs a driver's judgment. Some years ago, I drove continuously from New York to Minnesota. By the time I reached my destination, I was so dazed and tired that I drove through a stop sign without noticing it—though a policeman did. Like a fatigued driver, a weary dreamer wants to quit or shortcut the dream.

Let's balance our strength with the demands on us by increasing our "counter electromotive force" this way:

This is what the Lord Almighty, the God of Israel, says: . . . I will refresh the weary and satisfy the faint.[5]

[Jesus said,] Come to me, all you who are weary and burdened, and I will give you rest. Take my yoke upon you and learn from me, for I am gentle and humble in heart, and you will find rest for your souls. For my yoke is easy and my burden is light.[6]

The healthy answer for a tired driver is not in a prescription a druggist dispenses but in taking time to pull over to stretch, to eat, to rest. The empowering answer for a weary dreamer is found in the renewing strength that comes from the Creator and Sustainer of dreamers—God himself!

Here are eleven practical tips for effectively handling weariness:

1. Schedule daily time for prayer and meditation.
2. Make a weekly commitment to take a personal Sabbath. We are all "wired" differently, so rest may mean different things to each of us, but we all need rest. That is the reason God ordained a Sabbath rest. I use my day as a time to dream.
3. Help someone else who is weary finish a project you find interesting or would enjoy.
4. Take a nap regularly.
5. Once a month, have a "pamper yourself" day.
6. At the end of each day, take a thirty-minute emotional "vacation" (watch the sunset, listen to music, read a book, etc.).
7. Write down everything you are thankful for. (Put it in a letter and send it to a friend or family member.)
8. Laugh heartily.
9. Work out, using your favorite exercise method.
10. Treat yourself to your favorite dessert.
11. Return to #1. Start and end your fight against weariness with prayer.

Loneliness

FINALLY, *LONELINESS CAN OVERWHELM* a dreamer's creativity, productivity, and drive. When dreamers feel isolated or cut off from other people, the anguish of loneliness slows down their dreams. As a result, their dreams are in danger of burning out entirely. Dreamers may feel lonely when "nondreamers" distance themselves or seem indifferent because they don't understand or agree with the dreamer's mission and motives. If this happens, a dreamer doesn't have to lose a dream to loneliness.

My favorite dreamer knew the most oppressive impact of loneliness. During the final hours of Jesus' life, he needed—but didn't get—the support of his closest friends. His toughest times were his loneliest. One of his closest friends, Judas, betrayed him; another friend denied he even knew Jesus.

Jesus felt the stranglehold and the bottomless agony of loneliness. In the midst of Jesus' battle with loneliness, he cried out, "My God, why have you forsaken me?" Though in his grief and pain he felt like it, Jesus was not abandoned. *No one ever is.* God hadn't forsaken him, and God enabled Jesus to rise above the anguish of loneliness. The Resurrection proved that God was not just the founder—but also the finisher—of the dream.

Earlier in this chapter, I referred to the verse in Hebrews 12:1—"Throw off everything that hinders . . ."—for removing the cracked insulation of poor thoughts and attitudes. The very next verse in Hebrews challenges us to "run with perseverance the race marked out for us. Let us fix our eyes on Jesus, the author and perfecter of our faith."[7] In these words is the key that unlocks the door to responsible, rewarding renewal. The first action to take is to RUN. Don't give up and sit down for a "pity party." Run hard to God, and confront your loneliness with the truth that God's friendship and companionship will see you through it. One person told me, "Never run to God and tell him how big your problem is, but run to your problem and tell it how big your God is."

Second, it is important to fix or lock in on the loneliness specialist, Jesus Christ. It is disastrous when an athlete takes his or her eye off the ball. It is equally disastrous for a lonely person to take his or her eyes off God. Try this: Find a painting of Christ and really focus on it for five minutes. Focus yourself—your understanding, not just your eyes—on it. Then seek out a person to befriend. Your loneliness is likely to disappear.

Our dream motors need continual maintenance and care if they are to keep running smoothly, empowering our dreams. We need to guard against those things that can freeze up or seize up our creativity and productivity. For the sake of our dreams, it's wiser to commit to preventive maintenance than to continually face the breakdowns that can burn out our dreams.

UNPLUGGING DRAINING APPLIANCES

LET'S GO BACK TO our electrical-circuit image. If the electricity goes off, some root problem needs to be checked out. Flipping the circuit breaker isn't the fix, unless something has been fixed. Maybe something needs to be unplugged!

If your dream is flickering or slowing down, you might be knocking your head against some creative blocks. In a great book about creativity, *A Whack on the Side of the Head*, Roger von Oech lists what he considers major obstacles for dreamers. Here are seven obstacles from his list:

1. The Right Answer
2. "That's Not Logical"
3. Follow the Rules
4. Be Practical
5. Avoid Ambiguity
6. Play Is Frivolous
7. "I'm Not Creative"[8]

Von Oech calls these obstacles. You might say that each is an excuse—a reason why a dream is not getting off the ground or dying on the vine, a reason why sufficient electric current isn't getting through the circuit. Let's look at each of these for what they really are: excuses rather than real reasons. Then examine your life and "unplug" any of these excuses you find; they're pulling power needlessly away from your dreams.

There's One Right Answer

IT IS SOMETIMES NECESSARY to break free from what we "know is right" if we are to discover something new. Optical illusions illustrate this truth. (Is it a wine goblet or a profile of two people facing each other nose to nose?) Think also in terms of a good riddle. The point may be obvious—but not at first, because we're thinking in one set pattern and ignoring others that are just as viable. In the end I smile, slap my palm to my forehead, and say, "Oh, I didn't think of it that way."

Jim Collins's story proves that fresh approaches can lead to doing even what seems impossible. Jim liked to climb for fun, but in 1978 he made climbing history. He was the first person to conquer Psycho Roof, a dangerous rock in El Dorado Canyon, a world-famous spot for climbing near Boulder, Colorado.

The route climbers had used for years had proved impossible to climb. What held everyone back was getting a perch on the lip at the top of the cliff. The angle at which the lip jutted out blocked the climbers' hands from getting a good grip, and the lip was just beyond any climber's reach. Jim's solution was to turn himself upside down and—while he hung on to the side of the cliff below the lip—hook his toe onto the lip. Using his toes like fingers, Jim made the impossible dream a reality.

Today's buzzword, it seems, is *paradigm*. The word comes from the Greek *paradeigma*, meaning pattern, example, or model. A paradigm, then, is doing or thinking about something in a way that is consistent with one's own patterns or parameters of "the way it is." But our own pattern or model is likely not the only, and may not be the best, way of looking at or doing something. Businesses today commit considerable sums of money to send their "associates" (another buzzword) to training seminars to help them break free of the stifling effects of paradigms.

It's difficult to shift or change our paradigms, but to move beyond what we're experiencing and how we're thinking today, we must make changes. Dreaming great dreams requires imagining beyond our present paradigms. It may be today's buzzword, but it's long been a principle for great dreamers.

In 1859, everyone knew there was one right answer to the question, "What do you get from an oil well?" Oil. That was it, clear and simple. Based on that answer, people assumed that anything coming from an oil well must be flammable and hazardous. But when chemist Robert Cheesbrough visited America's first oil-producing well, he noticed—and wondered about—a clear residue forming around the rods of the well pumps. He collected a sample, took it home, and performed some experiments with it. Cheesbrough eventually extracted a waxy substance from the residue and suspected it might have healing powers. He believed in it so strongly, in fact, that he tested the product on himself.

Cheesbrough tried to market his discovery, but the market wasn't ready; people feared the containers of a substance coming from an oil well would explode. Eventually, traveling around the countryside and giving out free samples, Cheesbrough was able to convince people of both the safety and usefulness of *petroleum jelly*.

Too often we get stuck on what we know, or we lose out on possible discoveries by locking ourselves into looking for the one right answer and ignoring other possibilities. Asking yourself and asking others, "How can I approach this? Now how else could I approach this?" can help you get past the obstacle of the right answer.

That Won't Work Because It's Not Logical

ISN'T IT LOGICAL AND reasonable to assume that anything heavier than air can't remain airborne for any extended length of time? Yes. No! The Wright brothers, among others, realized that the key to the possibility of flight wasn't a question of weight but of air pressure, lift, and thrust. Through a logical process that dug deeper than "superficial logic," they came to the conclusion that machines could fly. Effectively applying logic and reason in dreaming should begin with a basic question: "What is the real question here?" The next time you fly in a thousands-of-pounds aircraft, think about how logical it is.

I've Got to Follow the Rules

THIS IS THE COROLLARY to "There's only one answer." This excuse says that there is only one way to come up with the answer. Of course we *do* need to follow some rules; moral or ethical rules and some code of agreed-upon conduct are necessary in any society. But a dreamer may need to question some procedural rules, because following the same trail will take you to the same destination time and time again. Physics students re-creating an experiment all follow the same procedure given in the text because that will yield the desired—the same—results. But in the real world of research—especially in medical and communications technology—new "rules" are written every day because only new paths will take us to new destinations.

When Robert Fulton told Napoleon about his invention of a steamboat, Napoleon retorted, "Why would anyone want to make a ship sail against the wind and currents by purposely lighting a bonfire under her deck?" Dreamers may need to "light a fire under the deck," take a divergent path, or try a new procedure to realize their dreams.

I've Got to Be Practical

IN THE SENSE OF its first Funk and Wagnall's definition, "pertaining to or governed by actual use and experience," the word *practical* can be nothing more than a smoke screen for maintaining the status quo—an excuse. People often call "practical" whatever is familiar and secure.

Dreamers can be encouraged by a second definition of the word: "having reference to useful ends to be attained." If your dream attains a useful end, it is practical.

Most people know the name Florence Nightingale, the English woman generally regarded as the founder of modern nursing. But most people don't know that Florence was born into a life of luxury. When she was just seventeen, Florence felt God calling her to a life of service. She dreamed of going into nursing, but her family flatly rejected the idea, dismissing it as impractical and unfitting for a young woman of her social rank.

But Florence would not give up her dream. Fourteen years later, despite her family's continued objections, Florence traveled to Kaiserswerth, Germany, to gain nursing experience.

Following that training, Florence was so successful in managing a small hospital in Harley Street in London that the British government asked her to lead a group of 38 nurses into the thick of the Crimean War. Inadequate medical and living conditions, unbearably long hours, and jealousy on the part of doctors and officials would have made life miserable for most people and perhaps convince them to find a new dream. But Florence chose commitment to her dream above personal comfort, earning the respect and honor of the soldiers she served, the medical profession, the British government, and the world.

Florence Nightingale's dream certainly "attained useful ends," and so was eminently practical. Contrary to popular opinion, dreamers *are* practical people!

In the 1950s and 1960s, the only "practical" use of computers was in large businesses, universities, and the military. Thomas Watson, the founder of IBM, prudently stated that he believed there was a world market for, at most, five computers. But in the 1970s, two young men, Steve Jobs and Steve Wozniak, believed the computer had practical potential for personal use. Their dream—a dream that began in a garage—translated to more than two million Apple II computers sold by 1985 and opened the door to the age of the personal computer.[9] Their impractical notion was a practical success.

I've Got to Avoid Ambiguity

THE MORE I LEARN, the more I realize I don't know. No one has all the answers. *Ambiguity* means a statement or situation that can be variously interpreted. Ambiguity in its best sense, then, leaves open possibilities that, on the surface, may not indicate potential for success. When I first introduced the idea of developing a master-planned community of faith with something significant for everyone, children through adults, I was vague and ambiguous. But the initial ambiguity paved the way for greater clarity as we explored various interpretations of exactly what "something significant" might mean. Initial ambiguity gave a greater range of possibilities to choose from in determining what would become reality.

At the beginning of the book, I talked about the importance of planning and focusing one's dream. That's important, but I here balance that with this point: Ideas take time to "work." My mother-in-law is a wonderful baker. When she bakes bread, I practically start shaking like my dog, Dreamer, when he's waiting for a treat. Ideas are like bread dough: They need time to rise. If you poke around too much or constantly keep checking on it, dough will never rise. Neither will an idea. Like the yeast in bread dough, an idea can slowly grow into an incredible creation. I have learned this from some of the world's most gracious "idea people": Ideas require patience, persistence, and positive faith. And I'd add that ideas need time. In time, if it's a good idea, ambiguity will turn to clarity.

Play Is Frivolous

THE OLD ADAGE "All work and no play makes Jack a dull boy" is true. A day without some play is less energizing than it could be, because it is often during play that we are relaxed enough to allow our imaginations to work. People are created to function most efficiently, effectively, and excellently with a healthy balance of work and play in life.

Recess is scheduled in the school day because it allows children time to work off steam so that they can come back to class recharged and ready to learn and accomplish. The time you spend to take a walk, throw a Frisbee with the dog, shoot some baskets, work the daily crossword, or play a game with the kids may be your most productive time, too.

> People are created to function most efficiently, effectively, and excellently with a healthy balance of work and play in life.

I'm Not Creative

IF YOU'RE STARTING TO think, *This problem is beyond me; I'm just not creative enough to see it through*, think again!

Consider the story of a young man who was fired from his job as a newspaper reporter. He was told he lacked ideas and wasn't creative. He found another job—and lost that one too. Then in 1928, on a train heading back to Hollywood from his latest disappointment in New York, this young dreamer created the character of Mickey Mouse. Walt Disney went on to create a world of enchantment for millions of people. But Mickey wasn't an overnight success. It wasn't until the advent of sound in motion pictures, enabling Disney to make the first synchronized sound cartoon, that Mickey Mouse brought Disney a 1932 Oscar and the creative recognition he so deserved.

This man who had been told he lacked ideas was a man whom the legendary, enormously creative science fiction writer Ray Bradbury referred to as his hero. Had Walt Disney taken to heart that early unfavorable assessment of his abilities, Disneyland and Disney World would not exist today, nor would his classic animated films that have delighted audiences in every corner of the world. We would never enjoy the rejuvenation of a day at Disneyland or the visual, musical delight of *Fantasia*.

> ♫
> **Creativity can be developed and is, at least to some degree, a choice. God placed creativity in the core of every individual.**

Creativity itself is not a single ability but a combination of skills: a sensitivity to problems, an ability to generate multiple ideas and ideas "off the beaten track," flexibility in applying ideas or approaches, the ability to redefine, and the ability to fill in details. Creativity, viewed this way, may be basic to all learning.

Creativity can be developed and is, at least to some degree, a choice. God placed creativity in the core of every individual. Make a point of being your own teacher, telling yourself "I am creative" and applying the skills mentioned above in everyday situations.

I challenge you to believe in yourself even when others don't. Negative personal put-downs bring negative results. Such phrases as "I'm stupid," "I'm no good," "I'm clumsy," or "I'm not creative" plant ideas in our minds that become self-fulfilling.

If you're convinced you're not creative, I challenge you to think of—to write down—five problems (any problems) you've solved in the last year. How did you use creativity in your problem-solving methods?

If that's hard for you, think about how creative problem solving can help preserve life itself. In 1995, Air Force Captain Scott O'Grady spent six days hiding on the ground in hostile territory—cold, hungry, and alone, but looking for and believing in the smallest possibilities that kept him and his dream of rescue alive. Shot down over Bosnia, O'Grady flattened himself into the earth beneath bushes and covered the bare skin of his ears with his green flight gloves to render himself invisible to passing patrols. He existed on grass, leaves, ants, rainwater caught in plastic bags—and prayer. Scott's dream of rescue, coupled with his creativity in using what resources he had, helped keep him alive through his six-day ordeal, an ordeal that made possible a new growth of faith within him.

Others who have been prisoners of war have also found that, when life was stripped of all but the barest of essentials—and even when those bare essentials were in short supply—God opened their eyes to creative possibilities and gave them dreams that sustained their lives. You are creative! Look for ways to use the gift.

ULTIMATE RENEWAL

THE BOTTOM LINE FOR renewing both the dreamer and the dream comes down to three factors: *hope, faith*, and *love*. It's unwise to dismiss these often-heard words as powerless. Now this is a rough analogy, but if God—the source of our power—can be compared to a hydroelectric generating station, then hope, faith, and love are the turbines through which God moves to create that power flow within us. Though they are intertwined, let's explore them one by one.

Healthy hope is more than wishful thinking. *Hope* is defined as confident expectation—desire accompanied by expectation of fulfillment.[10] To hope is not the same as to wish, for wishing involves only desire.

Hope that renews is anchored in the message of Pope John Paul II, delivered in his book *Crossing the Threshold of Hope*. He expresses hope as the absence of fear, and faith as the ouster of fear. Without faith, there is no hope, no confident expectation. The grounds for that hope, for the God-inspired dreamer, is the character of God. The Bible puts it this way:

> Put your hope in the LORD, for with the LORD is unfailing love and with him is full redemption.[11]

Hope is renewal for every dreamer and dream. *Where there is hope in the future, there is power to dream big dreams in the present.*

If you feel hopeless today, you can find hope:

> Do you not know?
>> Have you not heard?
> The Lord is the everlasting God,
>> the Creator of the ends of the earth.
> He will not grow tired or weary,
>> and his understanding no one can fathom.
> He gives strength to the weary
>> and increases the power of the weak.
> Even youths grow tired and weary,
>> and young men stumble and fall;
> but those who *hope* in the LORD
>> will renew their strength.
> They will soar on wings like eagles;
>> they will run and not grow weary,
>> they will walk and not be faint.[12]

Faith is another essential component in renewing and powering your dreams. "You gotta believe" is more than a slogan. Believing helps us live our dreams with energizing enthusiasm so we don't "short out" with cynical attitudes and discouragement from people and circumstances around us.

Have you ever watched a sporting event where a team that seemed certain to win "choked" and lost the game? Maybe you've worked alongside people who worked as if they were *trying not to lose* their jobs instead of *making the most of themselves through* their jobs. When we lose faith, we lose power to live our dreams.

"Now faith is being sure of what we hope for and certain of what we do not see," the Bible states.[13] There's that faith-hope link again! This dynamic faith is more substantial and solid than the manufactured faith we sometimes try to pump up based on believing in ourselves, because the

> **Where there is hope in the future, there is power to dream big dreams in the present.**

source of dynamic faith is the God of the universe. Many motivational speakers and writers suggest that we are our own source of faith. That's a pretty small foundation, because we are just a tiny part of the universe. We didn't create it; God did. Recognizing God as the foundation of faith gives us faith big enough to empower big dreams.

When the faith to nourish our dreams comes from an unlimited power source, our dreams have unlimited potential. Knowing God is behind our God-inspired dreams gives us confidence in our dreams, no matter what goes on around us. The greatest dreamer ever to walk the face of planet Earth, Jesus Christ, said, "*Faith* can move mountains." God-empowered faith can move us toward our dreams.

In daily life, we all operate on a kind of intellectual faith. For example, we unconsciously reason, "Based on experience, I believe that chair will support my weight," so we sit down. We trust that the light will come on when we flip the wall switch, and we're surprised when it doesn't. We have to operate on that kind of intellectual faith to negotiate daily living. But that kind of faith alone isn't enough to help us hold on to a dream that seems impossible.

A friend lightheartedly told me of an incident that drove that point home to her. She and her family went to a local water park for a day of fun together. To keep their relationship strong, she and her husband each try to share in things the other likes to do, so she found herself standing at the top of a five-story water slide (aptly named "Kilimanjaro") that her husband was sure she'd enjoy plummeting down. "In point of fact," she confided, "I could at that moment think of any number of other things I'd rather have been doing, like floating on a raft in the wave pool."

But she respected their commitment to at least *try* what the other enjoyed, so she rattled off in her mind all the reasons she knew it was safe to let go of the hand bar and shoot down the slide: The slide was a trough, so she couldn't fall off accidentally; the water was shallow, so she wouldn't drown; there was a long ramp at the bottom to help her glide to a stop; small children were going down and enjoying it safely. But, she admitted, all those very sound reasons were not enough to help her to let go of the bar at the top of the slide. What got her down the slide was knowing that the one who loved her wouldn't ask her to do anything that put her in peril, and he had gone down the slide himself first. Looking to and trusting in who was waiting at the bottom, she crossed her legs, pointed her toes, and let go—and she's glad she did.

That is precisely why we shouldn't simply refer to God; we need to begin—and end—with God, in looking for and living out our dreams. On earth, Jesus knew anxiety and anguish and all the other emotions we deal with in daring to dream; he knows what you and I are facing now. Our confidence can be in him, the one who loves us most and has dared to dream before us.

Working with hope and faith is *love*. The kind of love that is most nourishing is defined in the Bible:

> Love is patient, love is kind. It does not envy, it does not boast, it is not proud. It is not rude, it is not self-seeking, it is not easily angered, it keeps no record of wrongs. Love does not delight in evil but rejoices with the truth. It always protects, always trusts, always hopes, always perseveres. Love never fails.[14]

Love expects and encourages the best. M. Scott Peck illustrates the incredible power of this truth in a story he entitles *The Rabbi's Gift*.[15] Peck tells of the abbot of a monastic order in imminent danger of dying out. In search of advice to help save his dying order, the abbot visited a rabbi known for his wisdom. But all the rabbi had to offer was the cryptic phrase, "The Messiah is one of you." Confused, the abbot returned to the monastery and reported the rabbi's words to the other brothers.

> ℰ𝒫
>
> **Love is a compelling, energizing, sustaining, powerful force in renewing both dreamer and dream.**

As the brothers pondered the meaning of these strange words in the days and weeks that followed, they began to look at one another differently, realizing the gifts and good, rather than the faults and flaws, in each other. The brothers even began to look at the potential within themselves, and in so doing began to treat each other with "extraordinary respect, on the off chance that one among them might be the Messiah. And on the off, off chance that each monk himself might be the Messiah, they began to treat themselves with extraordinary respect."

The change was so remarkable that the occasional visitors who happened by sensed something strangely compelling about the place. They returned to pray, to picnic, to meditate, and even—one by one—to join the brothers, until the monastery once again was vital and alive, " a vibrant center of light and spirituality in the realm."

Love does that. Love is a compelling, energizing, sustaining, powerful force in renewing both dreamer and dream.

Two dreamers who plugged into the renewing power of faith, hope, and love in their own lives and dreams are retired real estate developer James Rouse and Christian Community Development

Association Chairman John Perkins, pastor of Voice of Calvary Ministries. Both bring that power of renewal to the dying dreams of inner-city residents.

Through his philanthropic Enterprise Foundation, and with private and governmental grants, Rouse, his coworkers, and the people of West Baltimore's Sandtown-Winchester neighborhood are bringing job training, playgrounds, computers to their schools, new housing, drug rehabilitation programs, greatly reduced infant mortality rates, and, most important, hope where hopelessness prevailed. Renewal began with the compassion and commitment of one man—James Rouse—who saw the spent ruin of a neighborhood, plugged into the power of a God-inspired dream, and carried the current of new hope to people whose hope was on the verge of complete blackout.[16]

The Christian Community Development Association works for both spiritual and economic renewal, the "re-neighboring" of neighborhoods, through member organizations in cities all across the country. One such organization in Detroit's east side helped organize block clubs to combat crime—targeting drug dealers and prostitution—provide positive activities to young people, and refurbish buildings—all achieved without financial aid from the government. Block clubs may partner with interested churches through the Joy of Jesus adopt-a-block program, which links suburban families with block residents for activities ranging from Bible study and shared meals to fixing leaky faucets and building lasting friendships. It's a program where individuals see that they can make a lasting difference in their community.[17]

Do you need the power of renewal to reenergize your dream today? Renewal is the current that enables dreamers to recharge their dreams and to connect with other dreamers to help them empower their dreams as well. Inspect the insulation around your attitudes, thoughts, and character; check your connection to the true outlet of power, overhaul your motor, and repair any damage done by routine, weariness, criticism, comfort, or loneliness; and unplug unnecessary excuses. Let the energy of renewal keep you running effectively to reach your dreams.

SEVEN

⊗⊘

Rekindling a
Lost Dream

JOSEPH WAS SHAKING, PARTLY from fear, partly from the
cold in his dark cell, but mostly from a feeling of betrayal and
confusion that washed over him again and again. Why, when
he had believed so passionately that his dream was true? Why a second time? Could he have been so wrong to misread what seemed so
clear? Was God there at all? If he was, what could this possibly mean?

You've thought you had it bad—and perhaps you have—but
have you ever been left for dead in a dark, dusty pit, or wrongfully
accused and thrown into prison? Joseph had been, and he was
scared. (His story is told in the Bible.)

What he'd thought was a glorious dream had brought him only
catastrophe. It had seemed such a beautiful dream, but a dream easily misunderstood, even resented, by his own family. His eleven
brothers already knew Joseph was their father's favorite. As if the
honors heaped upon Joseph weren't enough, he'd had the gall to tell
his family that he dreamed the sun, moon, and eleven stars were
bowed down to him. The brothers didn't need any psychiatrist to
interpret that dream for them; what they needed was a plan to pluck
this proud peacock once and for all.

One day Joseph's father sent him into the countryside to see how
his brothers were handling the flocks. That's when the brothers saw
their chance. Their own words were, "Here comes the dreamer. Let's
kill him."[1] Before Joseph knew what was happening, they attacked
him, threw him into a dark pit, and left him there to die.

In that instant he believed his life was over—and his dream was, too. Why? Dreams aren't supposed to turn out that way! But Joseph had no idea of the danger and terror that lay ahead of him. Some of his brothers saw a chance to make a quick buck as well as get rid of Joseph forever, so they sold him as a slave to a caravan of foreigners. The sun, moon, and stars bow down to him? Ha! Now he was a slave, his life in the hands of strangers.

Despair, fear, confusion, a creeping darkness of heart, and probably more than a little anger replaced Joseph's now dead dream. With a future completely uncertain, every day he journeyed farther from home, and every day the hurt and rejection buried his dream deeper.

When they arrived in Egypt, Joseph was sold again, this time to an influential Egyptian. Joseph—though still a slave—eventually found a place of responsibility in the affairs of the household. But just when things began looking brighter, Joseph was slandered and thrown into prison. The spark of a dream that had begun to burn in him was extinguished—again. Was there no end to the cruel injustice and suffering he had to endure?

Even though the dream seemed dead to Joseph, to God it was still vitally alive. Joseph found out what every persevering dreamer knows: *God always fights for his dreams and dreamers!*

Since childhood, Joseph had dreamed that he would play a significant part in saving a nation. Now that ability to dream and a God-given gift for interpreting dreams brought Joseph his freedom and the respect of his new employer, the Pharaoh. Pharaoh put Joseph in charge of administering the resources and economy of Egypt. And this responsibility put him in a place and position where his dream could come true. Thanks to Joseph's interpretation of significant dreams, when drought ravaged the area, Egypt—under Joseph—was prepared.

But Joseph's family back home was not; they were starving. Jacob sent his sons to Egypt to attempt to buy food. They didn't realize the mighty prince they bowed down before was the brother they'd betrayed. Joseph's dream came true, and he saved his family and nation from starvation.

Joseph discovered that God had never abandoned him, even in those darkest times when his dream seemed totally forsaken. God held on securely to the dream Joseph thought was lost. That truth is real, not only for Joseph, but for you and me as well. Be assured that God always fights for his dreams and his dreamers.

Feel as if you've lost a dream? Know that God knows where all our dreams are. Not for one moment has God lost track of our dreams. If our dream is slipping or has slipped away, we must let God, the *initiator* of our dreams, also be the *interpreter* of our dreams as well as the *insurer* of our dreams.

GOD AS DREAM INITIATOR

GOD TAKES GREAT PLEASURE in helping us find and fulfill our dreams. God initiated in Mary a dream beyond anything she could have imagined. Mary was just a teenager when God sent her the greatest dream the world has ever known: God chose Mary to be the mother of his son. Her nation expected a mighty messiah—a king—to appear on the scene to save Israel, not a baby born to a common girl living in an obscure village.

When God planted the dream in her heart, Mary's joy overflowed, but she must have been filled with some trepidation, too. Mary wasn't married. And yet her fiancé accepted her and the child that was not his own. And then came the birth. Never before, and never since that night, has the sky blazed with angels announcing a birth—a confirmation of how spectacular Mary's dream was. Other events confirmed that Jesus was God's Son, the promised Messiah.

> We must let God, the *initiator* of our dreams, also be the *interpreter* of our dreams as well as the *insurer* of our dreams.

Grown to manhood, Jesus attracted enormous crowds. Wherever he went, the blind received sight, the deaf heard, the sick got well. Jesus left a trail of people, once despairing and defeated, renewed into bold, confident dreamers.

Jesus was not on a mission to simply reinterpret the world; he came to change it, forever. God's dream for Jesus was to be more than a philosopher; he was to be the Savior.

He changed doubt to hope.
He changed hate to love.
He changed distress to peace.
He changed fear to faith.
He changed dullness to adventure.
He changed unhealthy self-image to healthy self-worth.

What must Mary have felt as she learned of the miracles her son was performing, heard the wisdom of his teaching, saw the crowds that followed him? Often her thoughts must have turned back to that day she first learned of God's dream for her life.

But Mary's dream became a nightmare. Popular opinion and religious and civil leaders united against Jesus. His life was in danger. Why?

And then Jesus was arrested. Had God abandoned her and his dream as well? Mary's heart was breaking. Certainly Jesus would be found innocent. But Jesus was sentenced to a criminal's death, crucified between two thieves. Friday—the day of his execution—came. As Jesus died, the sky turned black and the ground shook. Was the dream dead, too? Aghast, totally numbed and yet painfully pierced by grief, uncomprehending, Mary believed it was.

All the human signs pointed to a dream destroyed. In fact, Jesus' last words were, "It is finished." What was finished?

Thank God it wasn't the dream! The good news was that the dream wasn't dead at all; even death couldn't kill God's dream to save the world. Jesus defeated death by literally rising to life three days after he was buried. What a miraculous dream come true!

Mary saw Jesus alive again, and the dream that was ignited thirty-three years earlier became a blaze. God didn't destroy the dream or break a promise—he never has, and he never will. God sustains the dreams he inspires, and he can breathe life back into the embers of your dream today.

Mary's dream story did happen. And because it did, God's resurrection power is available to renew every dreamer and to rekindle every dream. God can initiate his dream for you—in you—right now. Receive it and live it!

GOD AS INTERPRETER

THE EIGHTEENTH-CENTURY ENGLISH POET William Cowper reflected on the truth that Joseph in Egypt and, centuries later, Mary in Nazareth discovered: God's ways are not our ways. I wonder what perplexity Cowper pondered when he wrote:

> God moves in a mysterious way
> His wonders to perform. . . .
> God is his own interpreter,
> And he will make it plain.

We don't—and *can't*—know what God knows, because God is not bound by time or space or our own physical constraints. So we can't know *how* God will work—only *that* God will work—to make the deepest dreams he inspires in us come to be. The other certainty that we as dreamers can hold fast to is that God's dreams are always for our good.

That's important to remember when the path you've set out upon seems to lead to a dead end or take you away from the direction of your dreams. God is not a one-idea God; he may have an alternate route that's better or wiser for you to take to reach your dreams. Don't think God is bound by your understanding or limitations.

A Detour Means There's More Than One Way

IF YOU'RE READY TO throw up your hands because you're hitting a roadblock, consider the possibility that God is nudging you to hold on to your dream but not your preconceived notions of how that dream should work out. Let me explain: As our church started growing rapidly, it became evident that we'd soon outgrow our fourteen acres. I looked for more land where we could expand and found that hundreds of acres were for sale only one block away from our site.

The state of Arizona owned the land, so I made an appointment to visit with a state land staff person. The meeting began when he walked briskly into the room as if he was in a hurry to get it over with. Bluntly he said, "I heard you wanted to buy some of our land. Do you have any money?"

I replied that I was only there to find out all the details for my church board. With that he stood up indignantly and told me the land was too expensive for us and I shouldn't have bothered him. Then he abruptly walked out.

I was stunned and humiliated. I felt like less than a zero. In my agonizing walk to the car, my mind replayed what had just happened. *Maybe I don't belong here,* I thought. *Who am I to think there would ever be any way for us to buy two hundred acres of prime land?*

But the dream to build a new church on a big enough site still tugged at me. Yes, I was disappointed and *confused,* but I *refused* to be discouraged. Fortunately, I didn't abandon the dream. Certainly God had not, and he had other means to work it out. Just a few years later, the mayor called and told me about some exceptional land located in one of the best spots in the city. It was a much better location than the first site! I checked it out and, after much negotiation and pursuit, we bought it. Thankfully, we didn't have to settle for something good, only to miss out on the best.

I love a line written by Wally Amos. Amos saw his dream come true in founding the successful cookie company that bore his name. But through a complicated series of mistakes, Amos lost not only the company but also the right to use his own name and likeness in any new business venture. That dream was swept away from him, but Amos was not swept away with it. In the midst of the challenges and disappointments, Amos discovered that he wasn't "dealing with a one-idea God." What a great line! We don't have a one-idea God.

Facing the loss of his dream, Amos widened his dream. He envisioned helping other dreamers by sharing what he'd learned through his experience, so he spoke at motivational seminars. He made a commitment to keep participating in charitable organizations and community projects. As a result of that work, Wally received an honorary doctorate in education from Johnson and Wales University, the Horatio Alger Award, and other prestigious honors.

Wally is thankful for what he learned along the way; notably, he has a new understanding of faith. And he believes with complete confidence that "my life and this mission are part of a journey; my prize is the road, not the goals."[2]

Wally found what many other dreamers have discovered, too: In the journey of living out dreams, our reward is not so much in the fulfillment of our dreams as it is in who we become and how we grow along the way.

> In the journey of living out dreams, our reward is not so much in the fulfillment of our dreams, as it is in who we become and how we grow along the way.

Finding Creative Options

WHEN FACING A DREAM that seems lost, God may ask us to "see the big picture" and look for creative options. To find a lost dream, a dreamer may need to branch out, to increase his or her skills. In a previous chapter, we talked about a dreamer's mind-set. Think now in terms of a skill-set.

Our friends' camping cookbook lists ten different ways to start a fire and four different ways to stack wood to build a fire. When your dream seems to falter, look for new skills within you and new ways to apply the skills you have to reach your dream.

Sometimes new options open when you look for an extension of the talents and skills you're already applying. Famed pianists Christoph Eschenbach and Vladimir Ashkenazy and renowned cellist Mstislav Rostropovich successfully turned the skills of interpretation and technique that had made them internationally acclaimed performers to a new venture—conducting. Not everyone can become an acclaimed musician, and not all skills translate so clearly to another venture, but everyone has some talents, skills, and imagination. When we intentionally enhance and improve our talents, they become skills. As we apply our skills, we make dream discoveries and generate dream ideas. Some practical ways to develop a dream mind-set and skill-set:

- Listen to what is being said through your *imagination* ears instead of through your *information* ears. Information tells you what is; imagination tells you what can be.
- Look at what you see through *innovative* eyes instead of through *status quo* eyes. Look beyond the obvious.
- Drink in as much as you can from different dream "wells," because your dream will never run dry if you are willing to drink from different wells. Look for new sources. Learn from people who have been successful in areas outside the area of your dream.
- Get reality checks on your skills from trusted friends, then do something every day to improve those skills until the day you die.
- Attend seminars, workshops and classes, watch video presentations, listen to tapes, and travel to inspiring places where dreams are actually being lived out.
- Find a mentor who shares your core values and can give you insight and information.

Sometimes an abrupt change in our circumstances leads to discovering entirely new options. In 1936, following a serious auto accident, young naval officer Jacques Cousteau began swimming daily in the Mediterranean to recover strength in his arms. To spare his eyes from the saltwater, another officer gave Cousteau a pair of pearl-fisherman's goggles, and his "eyes were opened on the sea." Captain Cousteau wrote, "Sometimes we are lucky enough to know that our lives have been changed, to discard the old, embrace the new, and run headlong down an immutable course."[3]

> ꙮ
>
> **Innovative eyes assess what we *have*—not what we *lack*—and look for new ways to apply talents or resources to reach our dreams.**

Innovative eyes assess what we *have*—not what we *lack*—and look for new ways to apply talents or resources to reach our dreams. Jim Tunney, former National Football League referee, tells the story of a youngster at the California State Special Olympics. The boy had cerebral palsy and couldn't use either hand. He had use of only one of his legs. Competing in a wheelchair race, the boy couldn't move himself forward with just one leg, so he turned his wheelchair around, pushed himself backward, and won the race.[4]

Never take lightly the ideas, options, and discoveries that emerge as you activate and apply your skills and as you look for new ways to apply your skills when obvious doors close.

GOD AS INSURER

A FRIEND OF MINE recently lost the diamond from her engagement ring. In her search for the missing stone, God showed her an important truth about us and our dreams. She told me:

> When I looked down and saw an ugly black hole where that brilliant diamond had been, my heart sank. Where and when did I lose it, and however would I *begin* to know where to look for it? I mentally checked off all the things I'd done

that day that might have dislodged a loose stone. Washing my hands? I checked the bathroom sink, floor, and wastebasket. No stone. Getting dressed? I went through the bedroom with my nose to the floor. No stone. Then it hit me: I'd given up on the sickly ivy hanging in the bathroom and transplanted it to the planter box on the porch.

My heart rose and plunged at the same time. I'd moved two other plants in the planter box and tossed some of the extra potting soil on yet another plant. As I began to sift the soil out on newspapers, I realized it was full of small pieces of quartz. The diamond wasn't large; it was just twenty points. It would be like looking for a needle in a box of pins. All I had going for me was the fact that my diamond wasn't shaped like an ordinary rock—that, and my determination to find it.

Through the painstaking search, she realized *what* made that small stone valuable.

It wasn't the DeBeers empire that sets the price of diamonds. I knew our homeowners' insurance would cover the monetary loss. What made it valuable was the love that bought it. And I thought immediately of the love that bought me— Jesus. If I was looking this hard for the sake of what love bought, how much harder does God "look" for us when we're lost? If my husband's dream for our marriage—represented by that small stone—mattered enough to me that I'd pour over rotting leaves and worm castings to find it, how much further will God go to help us find our dreams when we feel they're lost? They're never lost to God.

The happy ending is that my friend did find her missing stone, a tiny chip sparkling in the dirt and decay. You may feel your dream is a tiny speck, irretrievably lost, but God knows where it lies. For the sake of his love that bought you and your dream, God will work tirelessly to help you find your God-inspired dream—and finish it. The apostle Paul told the Philippians he was confident that he who began a good work in you will carry it on to completion, [5]

for it is God who works in you to will and to act according to his good purpose.[6]

Once again we need to remember that God is the initiator, interpreter, and insurer of our dreams.

WHERE'S THE LOST AND FOUND DEPARTMENT?

IF YOU THINK EVERYTHING else has failed, don't despair. Turn to prayer.

In a business office high above the crowded streets of New York, one man sat intently listening to another who was emotionally pouring out his problem. He was about to lose everything he'd spent his life dreaming about and working for. The two tried to step back and reason for a while, looking at all the angles, searching for solutions. Finally, in desperation, the dejected man sighed, "There's nothing more that can be done."

His friend countered, "That's not true. There is something else that can be done. We can pray." This answer astonished his friend, who admitted that he didn't even know how to pray. But there in the office, they talked with God just the way they had been talking and listening to each other. In that moment when all seemed lost, they invited God—the greatest problem solver and greatest power in the world—to take charge of the dream's risks, rewards, and responsibilities.

Picture prayer as the "lost and found" department—the first and best place to check for lost dreams. Anyone who has ever dreamed big dreams has almost certainly experienced failure along the way. Prayer plays a vital role in positively managing failure by placing it in the hands of the one who can manage it best: God. We can never know enough or do enough to eliminate the possibility of failure from our lives. Perhaps we shouldn't even seek to, for God can bring constructive, positive results from what we consider failure. Prayer keeps failure from being final or fatal.

I've experienced this personally. In 1984, the president of our congregation and I had to release ten out of twenty staff members. On top of that, we had to inform the ten remaining staff members that they would receive a 25 percent pay cut, effective immediately. My feelings of failure turned to tears, and those tears turned into prayers. I cried out to God that the dream of building a dynamic church was failing. Then God reminded me that I was not in the position to make that judgment. Only God knew what the future looked like. The best thing I did was to take the dream to him in prayer.

Imagine what God foresaw in 1984: a strong, healthy, vibrant mission center with a full- and part-time staff of one hundred by 1994, with a worldwide outreach. I had confused my temporary *feelings* of failure with the permanent *facts*. Through prayer, God carried me through my feelings and provided everything we needed to get us, and the dream, where we are today. God promises the same for you. You can talk with him now through prayer and begin to find out for yourself.

FOUR STEPS TO MOVE FORWARD

RIGHT NOW, ANY PERSON who has lost their dream can retrieve the dream by taking four practical steps:

Believe!

BELIEVE THE DREAM IS still alive, even though it seems lost. Believe that great dreams never die. Believe that God can show you where to go and what to do.

Jesus said,

I tell you the truth, if you have faith as small as a mustard seed, you can say to this mountain, 'Move from here to there' and it will move. Nothing will be impossible for you.[7]

When things looked grim, Linda had the faith to believe. Linda was living out her dream as a wife, mom, and good citizen—but then her world crashed with an unexpected divorce. To ease the pain,

Linda turned to alcohol, which only took her lower into the depths of suffering.

Then one day, a friend invited Linda to an Alcoholics Anonymous support group. There Linda admitted her need for God's help. This first step along her journey of faith was reinforced when she went on a spiritual retreat.

Linda, once despairing of life, found life—and the road to success. As a businesswoman, she was recently named Woman of the Year by the Arizona Press Association. As Linda shared her story of faith with me, I was captivated by her enthusiasm. She talked about her faith as if she were talking about her very best friend. Her excitement about how faith helped her dream again was contagious. Linda learned firsthand that believing—faith—can move mountains.

Receive!

RECEIVE GUIDANCE, DIRECTION, AND help. God tells us that what is impossible with us is possible with him. Instead of wasting energy in trying to get God's attention, be open to the reality that God is trying to get your attention. You never have to convince God to care about your needs; God will eagerly give us what we need. All we have to do is receive.

Ask for and listen to encouragement. And ask for and listen to positive help.

Many months ago, I again felt as if a dream might be slipping away. We had been working hard to raise the $3.2 million needed to buy the orange grove I mentioned earlier, where our congregation would build. The money wasn't coming in, but negative voices were. People made unkind comments. At the point where the dream seemed lost, I went to a meeting where my good friend Robert Schuller was also in attendance. He could see I was struggling. Briefly, I shared some of my pain. Then he took hold of my shoulders, looked me squarely in the eye, and said, "I believe in you and your dream!"

I was so moved that I almost started to cry. That was exactly what I needed to keep me going. If your dream is slipping from you, seek out the company of positive people who can help you see beyond the current mire you're in.

Achieve!

IF EVERYWHERE WE LOOK we see only one acceptable method, course of action, or attitude, it becomes difficult when we feel a dream has slipped away to achieve the possible, the uncommon, the extraordinary.

In faith, step out and do something that will activate your lost dream. Mary Kay Ash, founder of Mary Kay Cosmetics, always begins the day with her list of six things that are most important to her that day. She tackles the list in order of priority. Every dreamer needs a "to do" list every day. Every dream needs to be acted on.

Do *something* that will move you in a positive direction. Something. Unless they are carving something the size and scale of Mount Rushmore, sculptors don't rely on jackhammers and dynamite to bring their vision into being. While an artist working in stone may initially remove large sections to rough out the basic shape of a piece, it is the many smaller chips made by hammer and chisel that finally shape a piece to its finished form. Each cut, great or imperceptible, affects the final shape. Each cut is important.

Praise!

REKINDLING OUR LOST DREAMS does require much from us, but my friend Lloyd Ogilvie told me, "Whatever you do, Walt, don't miss the joy!" We were designed to live with joy. Praise produces joy. The Bible says:

> We also rejoice in our sufferings, because we know that suffering produces perseverance; perseverance, character; and character, hope. And hope does not disappoint us, because God has poured out his love into our hearts by the Holy Spirit, whom he has given us.[8]

Do you need a breath of fresh air to sweep over the dying embers of your dream today? In the time of the ancient Hebrews, wind was referred to as "*ruach*," which means "breath of God." Perhaps you need to let God's breath fan your dream fires. Martin Luther said:

> Everything that is done in the world is done by hope. No farmer would sow one grain of corn if he hoped not it would grow up and become seed; . . . no merchant or tradesman would set himself to work if he did not hope to reap the benefit.

Hope plays a surprisingly powerful role in dealing with both problems and possibilities. Hope contributes to better performance, more excellent health, happier relationships, and greater dream realization. And researchers offer hope: Optimism can be developed and nurtured.

No one would have blamed Bernie Marcus and Arthur Blank for thinking it was the end of the world when, in 1978, they were fired from their jobs with Handy Dan, a do-it-yourself hardware retailer. Neither of them came from affluent circumstances: Marcus's father was a poor Russian cabinetmaker in New Jersey, and Blank was a one-time juvenile gang member from a lower-middle-class neighborhood in Queens. A friend who was an investor encouraged them to see this setback as a golden opportunity, and the result was the beginning of a giant in the home-improvement industry, Home Depot.

Marcus says he now asks other successful entrepreneurs if there was ever a time in their lives when despair was a major factor. Eighty percent of those he's asked have responded yes, but go on to say that they looked at their setbacks as positive experiences.[9] Hope makes that possible.

HOPE IS THE MAGNET THAT DRAWS US TO OUR DREAMS

I REMEMBER SEVERAL YEARS ago reading an article in *Newsweek* that told how a five-year-old boy, Rocky, helped save his mother's life. Rocky and his mother were riding together when their vehicle flipped over and rolled down a deep ravine. Rocky's mother, needing immediate medical attention, was blinded by blood running down her face.

Crawling out of the car and up the ravine took every ounce of energy the woman had. Halfway up the slope, she wanted to give up. But Rocky reminded her of the story *The Little Engine That Could*: "I think I can, I think I can, I think I can." Rocky pulled and called out encouragement, and they made it up to the highway, where a passing motorist rushed them to a hospital.

That kind of powerful, relentless, dogged hope that won't give up is what locates lost dreams and launches new dreamers. Do you have hope? God has a great enough supply for everyone to have more than they need. All you need to do is to go to the source of hope, in prayer, and receive it.

Recently I went on a personal tour of McDonald's "Hamburger University" in Oakbrook, Illinois. My tour guide, Marci, was showing me the highlights when she suddenly stopped and remarked, "Ray Kroc had more setbacks than people realize."

> *Do you have hope? God has a great enough supply for everyone to have more than they need.*

I responded by saying that Mr. Kroc, the founder of McDonald's, mastered one of the most important lessons anyone can learn: He believed his dream was possible.

One big challenge Ray Kroc encountered in the early days of his very first McDonald's restaurant was what he labeled "The Great French Fry Flop." Though he followed the same procedure used by the McDonald brothers after he bought their highly successful restaurant in San Bernardino, California, Ray's first efforts failed to reproduce the delectable French fries that were a key part of the business. But Ray persisted, contacted experts at the Potato and Onion Association, and devised a system for curing potatoes that produced a fry that actually exceeded his expectations.

A $400,000 financial setback could have spelled the end of McDonald's before it really got off the ground. But Ray and his fellow dreamer, Harry Sonneborn, forged ahead with a plan and borrowed the money from their suppliers. This action not only saved the fledgling company from bankruptcy but also forged bonds of mutual support with the suppliers—in fact, strengthening the company. Ray stated that the success from this setback gave them the courage it took to borrow again and enabled McDonald's to rapidly expand.

"Adversity can strengthen you if you have the will to grind it out," Ray stated with assurance.[10] Ray came back from these and other setbacks strongly enough to lay the foundation for an enterprise that was the nation's most profitable retailer from 1984 through 1994. In 1994, McDonald's was opening an average of three new locations every twenty-four hours.

WHEN THE WAY IS DARKEST, REACH UP

AUDREY, WHO WORKS AT Community Church of Joy, knows firsthand about the dark valleys of lost dreams. Years ago, her five-year-old daughter, Michelle, became very sick. Michelle was diagnosed with a brain tumor. The tumor was malignant, and, not long after, Michelle died.

On one of the nights Audrey spent looking down the corridor of the hospital, she saw through her tear-filled eyes a silhouette of a figure that looked like Jesus. Warm light radiated from the figure. His face, Audrey could see, was gracious, and he looked at her with beautiful, loving eyes. Peace enveloped her, and Audrey knew she was not alone.

Just a short time later Audrey's husband died in a freak accident at work. Following that, her mother died of a heart attack. Close on the heels of that sorrow, Audrey learned that her young brother had lung cancer. Audrey shared with me that, if she hadn't had her eyes on Jesus Christ, there would have been no way she could have survived all those blows to one dream after another. Audrey perseveres, believing that God's will for her is good, receiving the comfort and guidance God has extended freely to her through Jesus, stepping out to achieve the dreams God is working to complete through her life, with a heart full of praise.

EIGHT

⁂

The Art of Dream Building

IN AN EARLIER CHAPTER, I cited Robert Schuller's great line: "Build a dream and the dream builds you." That's true. And so is this: Build a dream and the dream builds dreams for others. Let me illustrate what I mean.

A few years ago, sociologist Virginia Satir accepted the challenge of working with a group of people on public welfare. Her personal goal was to help participants realize that they all had the capacity to achieve and to become more self-sufficient. Every Friday, for three hours, Satir met with the group—racially diverse and living in a variety of family systems.

On her first Friday night, Satir asked a fundamental question, "What are your dreams?" The response was almost hostile. One person snapped, "Dreams? I don't have dreams." She explained that she couldn't dream very well when rats were eating her children's food.

Calmly and courageously, Satir persisted. "Tell me why the rats are eating your children's food." The woman said her screen door was broken and needed repair. Satir then asked if anyone in the group was handy enough to fix a screen door. One man spoke up, saying that he had a dream to become a fix-it man. Satir handed him some cash to buy material to fix the hole-ridden screen door.

By the next week, the fix-it man had repaired the screen door, and Satir once again asked the group to share its dreams. The first comment came from the woman who now had a rat-proof screen door. The words poured out. She dreamed of becoming a secretary,

149

but she had six children to take care of. Satir asked if anyone in the group could take care of six children for a few days a week while this woman got some secretarial training.

Another woman volunteered that *her* dream was to become licensed to care for children; she agreed to help get her own dream going by caring for the six children. A similar scenario continued. And within twelve weeks everyone in Satir's group was able to get off public welfare. Confidence and self-respect soared.[1] In this group and repeatedly since this experience, Satir was a dream builder. She inspired people to transform their thoughts into actions, energizing others to dig for their own dreams. What's more, each person was a dream builder for another.

Our dreams can—they *do*—impact other people; they impact our relationships. Dreams are not simply abstract; dreams are relational. The more adventuresome the dream, the more it challenges us and others.

> ✑
>
> **The more adventuresome the dream, the more it challenges us and others.**

The dream that caught fire in Roy Thomas's mind eventually fueled a dream that seemed unreachable for a young boy on the other side of the world. An African-American struggling against both racial prejudice and financial hardship, Roy had a family that encouraged him to dream, to go to college, then medical school. As a young surgeon, Roy served as an officer in the Army in Korea, where in 1955 he met Yang-chin Chi, a young man working as a domestic servant but dreaming of a better life and an education.

Yang-chin Chi knew of struggle himself. Ten years earlier, tuberculosis had wiped out both his father and his family's savings. Any hopes for his own education seemingly vanished when North Korean troops had crossed the border in 1950. In flight, his family had sought refuge on bleak Soonwee Island. In 1952, not yet 16, Chi had been separated from his family when they again fled from North Korean troops.

After the war, Chi ended up in Il-dong, north of Seoul, where he found work at a military base. And there Chi met Captain Roy Thomas, stationed there as surgeon and chief medical officer. Roy befriended Chi, helping him with his English, encouraging his aspirations, learning about his life—as Chi learned of Dr. Thomas's own struggles and accomplishments.

Hoping to find a way to make his dream come true, Chi eventually moved to Seoul, working as a waiter at an officers' club. Unable to save any money, Chi began to despair of his dream until one day when Dr. Thomas appeared at the club. Thomas took the time to drive Chi to Seoul National University so he could better envision the possibility of one day being a student. Thomas reiterated his belief in Chi and Chi's dream of a college education.

When Thomas returned to America, he continued to write to Chi, encouraging him, prodding him to take a university entrance exam. Thinking it was a useless exercise, Chi finally took the exam for Chung-Ang University, passing with high marks. But other obstacles remained: Lacking the eighty-five dollars for tuition, Chi wrote a despairing letter to Dr. Thomas.

Six weeks later Chi opened a letter from Dr. Thomas that had eighty-five dollars tucked inside.

Dr. Thomas's encouragement and gift paved the way for Yang-chin Chi to graduate from Chung-Ang University. What's more, Chi later won a Fulbright Scholarship and earned a master's degree from the University of Wisconsin and a Ph.D. in social work from the University of Sussex, in Brighton, England. Where is Chi now? He is a professor at Chung-Ang University.[2]

I tell this story to illustrate the power of one person's dream to build another person's dream. Whether he set out to be or not, Dr. Thomas was a dream builder.

What is a dream builder? Dream builders help people perceive more than they ever dreamed they would see, believe more than they ever dreamed possible, and experience more than they ever dreamed they would know. You might say that dream builders build dream fields.

BUILDING DREAM FIELDS

LET'S CONSIDER A DREAM of a writer named W. P. Kinsella. What if an Iowa corn farmer built a baseball field in the middle of his cornfield and called it a "field of dreams"? On that field a father and son, one of whom was dead, would be reunited one last time for a game of baseball.

Kinsella developed this dream into a novel entitled *Shoeless Joe*. The novel, in turn, caught the attention of film director Phil Robinson, who transformed it into the movie *Field of Dreams*. The movie, starring Kevin Costner, was a dream-come-true success, receiving a nomination for an Academy Award.

Kinsella's idea for a "field of dreams" didn't just get on paper and film and end there. Something took root in the heart and on the land of Don Lansing, the farmer in Dyersville, Iowa, who owns the cornfield in which the movie was filmed. Today thousands of people come to this field to sightsee, to play a little baseball, to get married, or simply to dream.[3]

It might seem that Kinsella's dream had run its course, but like a pebble dropped in water, the ripples of its inspiration continued to grow, generating still more dreams. I received a newspaper clipping of a story about a father and his seventeen-year-old son. They had been reunited that very week—for the first time since the boy's birth. And where did the reunion take place? In Don Lansing's cornfield.

W. P. Kinsella . . . Phil Robinson . . . Don Lansing . . . a real-life father-son reunion and many other reconciling reunions of the heart—from one man's dream, one book, countless other dreamers found inspiration, delight, comfort, and their own dreams. One dream's ripples can stir an entire ocean of opportunities.

Dreams are like kaleidoscopes with their myriad of diverse patterns that shift and flow from a simple turn of the tube. The first time I looked at the end of a kaleidoscope, I was surprised by how few pieces of glass were there. From those few pieces came endless designs, all built upon the same material. A great dream is the same; from it, given a "turn" from another dreamer, countless exquisitely different dreams can come.

Build a dream. The beauty of the design you will find as your dream unfolds will encourage you to keep dreaming, and it can help others—and you yourself—to envision new dreams with new patterns engendered by your dream's design.

LIVING YOUR OWN DREAM AS A MODEL FOR OTHERS

WHEN YOU BEGIN LIVING out your dream, you will be an encouragement to others to live out their dreams. The most powerful persuasion for ourselves and for others comes not from what we say but from what we do.

When I pursued my dream to get a doctorate in theology, Lolly, one of our staff counselors, saw what I was doing. Lolly told me she was so encouraged by watching me live out my dream that she decided to pursue hers: going for a doctorate in clinical psychology. To do so Lolly had to relocate to the edge of adventure. Lolly had to rearrange her schedule at home and at work. Instead of waking up at seven in the morning, her alarm went off at five. That early in the morning, she poured herself into her doctoral studies. She had to reduce her work schedule, but she delighted in the change, even though her income dropped accordingly. Lolly refocused and found creative resources to cover her family's needs, even though both Lolly and her husband, Matt, were contributing to their son's college tuition and support.

Building my own dream helped inspire Lolly to build hers. Today she is Dr. Lolly Pisoni.

JESUS AS OUR MODEL DREAM BUILDER

IN THE BIBLICAL ACCOUNT of Jesus' life, I see the son of God as the ultimate dream builder, encouraging others to dream, and transforming dreams. Jesus had an impact on everyone he met. He transformed the dreams of some fishermen, once intent on filling their nets, but eventually eager to change the world. Jesus changed the lives of prostitutes, tax collectors, poor people, rich people. The Bible confirms this: "People recognized Jesus. They ran throughout that whole region and carried the sick on mats to wherever they heard he was."[4]

Blind people who dreamed to see—saw
Deaf people who dreamed to hear—heard
Crippled people who dreamed to walk—walked
Hungry people who dreamed to eat—ate
Lonely people who dreamed of friends—found friends
Anxious people who dreamed of peace—found peace
Addicted people who dreamed of transformation—were transformed

Jesus was more than a builder of dreams: He was a fulfiller of great dreams. You and I are invited to be "little Christs" to the blind, deaf, lame, hungry, restless, and addicted. Jesus himself said:

I tell you the truth, anyone who has faith in me will do what I have been doing. He will do even greater things than these, because I am going to the Father. And I will do whatever you ask in my name, so that the Son may bring glory to the Father. You may ask me for anything in my name, and I will do it.[5]

> If we build our dreams on the model Jesus gave, then living out our dreams will positively affect others in ways far beyond what we could imagine.

If we build our dreams on the model Jesus gave, then living out our dreams will positively affect others in ways far beyond what we could imagine, inspire others to envision new dreams, and give others a model for building their own dreams. It will change our lives profoundly for the better as well.

Explore with me some attitudes and qualities of sound dream builders.

DREAM BUILDERS GIVE PERMISSION TO DREAM

IN THE MOVIE *Dead Poets' Society,* the lead character, school teacher John Keating—played by actor Robin Williams—was a cheerleader for great dreams. In one scene, John takes a group of students down into the school lobby, home of a trophy case displaying pictures of past graduates. Keating points out that every one of the faces represents a dynamic dream.

Then he wonders aloud how many of these students, now grown men, actually lived out their dreams. Leaning toward the students gathered around him, Keating then whispers, *"Carpe Diem!"* Seize the day! They're cautious at first, but as the powerful challenge words sink in, the students are captured by the dream. Sometimes all we need is someone to encourage us and give us permission to dream God-inspired dreams.

John Keating gave permission to dream, but we need to remember that God gives the encouraging provision. You and I can also be a part of encouraging a dream's development and implementation process.

DREAM BUILDERS RESPECT DREAMERS

EVERY PERSON, SOMEWHERE IN his or her heart and mind, has—or has had—a dream. It is important, in helping other people build their dreams, to treat them like great dreamers with great dreams.

I am convinced that God's toughest job is making us believe that we are valuable. And God—the ultimate Dream Builder—asks us to help him do that job in building up one another.

Dallas Cowboys coach Jimmy Johnson notes a difference in the way some coaches treat their rookies. What was important, Johnson maintained, was understanding that *"whether* a player makes [is successful on] the team might hinge on something as subtle as *whether* you know his name and *whether* you treat him as an individual that you care about, with talent you believe in."6

Subtle, perhaps, but even such small gestures as paying enough attention to learn someone's name communicates the respect that builds a person's confidence.

Murray Smith, a sports psychologist who works with the Edmonton Oilers of the American Hockey League, sees the results of ridicule in some of the young men who actually do make it in professional hockey. "Some of these kids," he says, "finally get up there in the NHL and look across and see Gretzky or Lemieux and there's this feeling that they don't belong. Often the seeds for that have been planted long ago by adults telling them that they were no good, that they were stupid."[7]

You may know the proverb that states that it takes a thousand positive words to overcome one negative word. That's why it's so important for dream builders to speak out enthusiastically—sometimes with a shout.

Treating others as though they *already are* encourages them to *become* all they can be. In the musical *My Fair Lady*, Eliza Doolittle tells Professor Higgins's mother:

> I should never have known how ladies and gentlemen behave if it hadn't been for Colonel Pickering. He always showed me that he felt and thought about me as if I were something better than a common flower girl. You see, Mrs. Higgins, apart from the things one can pick up, the difference between a lady and a flower girl is not how she behaves, but how she is treated. I shall always be a flower girl to Professor Higgins because he always treats me as a flower girl and always will. But I know that I shall always be a lady to Colonel Pickering because he always treats me as a lady, and always will.[8]

No person with an idea is so dumb or so useless that he or she should be put down, which brings me to my next dream-building quality.

DREAM BUILDERS RESPECT DREAMS

WHENEVER A PERSON SHARES an idea with me, I treat it with the dignity and respect it deserves. The idea may not be practical or even feasible, but every idea may possess a valuable seed that can produce other ideas with the potential of one day improving the world.

What if we don't think the idea is a good idea? Every person needs to be valued; separating the value of a person from the value of his or her idea requires discernment. We need to be gracious as we affirm the person and *explore* the idea. Grace guides us to speak and act in a way that builds the other person up, even if the idea is not a good one. As Paul told the Christians in the town of Ephesus: "Do not let any unwholesome talk come out of your mouths, but only what is helpful for building others up according to their needs, that it may benefit those who listen."9

It is harder to respond out of grace than out of judgment. We seem to have a natural tendency to pick out the fault. From focusing on the one tiny white flake on an otherwise black sweater, picking out differences in a "What's wrong with this picture?" puzzle, to telling the optometrist which image is clearer, we live from one judgment to another.

Judgment seems to be conditioned into us. That's why as dream builders we need to temper our judgment with grace and continually check our words and actions to be sure they pass through this filter.

DREAM BUILDERS ARE LOYAL TO DREAMERS

A DREAM BUILDER WILL have the sense of a goose to stand by the dreamer, no matter what happens. Let me explain. Geese don't cover great distances by flying solo. They fly as a flock in a "V" formation—for good reasons. As it flaps its wings, each bird generates lift for the bird behind it, increasing the energy potential for the entire flock. Of course, this helps geese in the back of the lineup more than those in front. But the flock has a way to guard against the fatigue of the front flyer; when the lead bird tires, it falls back into the formation, and another bird takes over the front post. And why do geese honk as they fly? Birds in the back are encouraging the birds in front to maintain their speed. The group dynamics also apply when a goose is injured or ill; two geese will accompany an injured bird to the ground and stay with the goose until it is able to fly again or until it dies.

That kind of commitment to each other and to the goal makes it possible for geese to cover vast distances in their migrations. That kind of commitment to each other and to the dream makes it possible for dreamers and dream builders to dare to live out great dreams. Dream builders are loyal and faithful.[10]

DREAM BUILDERS ARE WILLING TO TAKE RISKS FOR DREAMERS

BEING A DREAM BUILDER costs us something. It may cost us in terms of our time, financial resources, or resources of thought or our abilities; it probably will cost us in terms of an emotional and spiritual investment if we care about the dreamer.

For many years, Martha Hawkins has run a restaurant called Martha's Place. And every day she thanks God for a lawyer named Calvin Pryor who was willing to invest something in her dream.

For years, she'd been telling people of her dream to one day open a restaurant—serving good food in the company of good people. She wanted customers to feel like they were coming to her house to share her finest meal. Martha admits that, for a long time, her dream seemed as far away as the moon.

Martha had married at sixteen and divorced at twenty-three, with four boys to raise. The daily strain of mothering, balancing finances, and long working hours finally affected her health; she developed kidney problems and suffered severely with a ruptured appendix. In desperation, Martha gulped down pills and more pills, eventually trying to end her life with an overdose; she awoke in a psychiatric hospital.

Following her recovery and release, Martha returned home to the housing project. Later, when her sons went to college, Martha occasionally brought a homemade meal to the dormitory—delighting the whole unit. Martha's dream kindled. When she cooked, she felt whole inside.

Then at work cleaning one day, Martha met Calvin Pryor. She told him about her dream of running her own restaurant. They kept talking. Pryor believed in her, and one day Pryor offered to make what Martha calls the "house of her dreams" available to her rent free until her business prospered. The sturdy old house required a lot of work—a "labor of love"—on the part of Martha, her family, and her friends, to bring it to opening day. But Martha's Place finally served its first customer, and it's been going strong ever since.

To Calvin Pryor and to Martha's family and friends, the risks they took as dream builders for Martha were worth the reward. No one should take dream building lightly. Dreamers and dream builders should have open eyes: Dreaming does involve risks. Of course, one should never invest or lend financially more than one can reasonably afford to lose, should something go wrong. An investment of time, thought, talent, emotions, and prayer is no less significant. Dream building is a commitment, but one whose rewards are most often worth the risks.

DREAM BUILDERS PRAY FOR DREAMERS

IN 1986, GUY DOUD was chosen the National Teacher of the Year. To Guy's mind, education includes helping mold God's dream for every individual—those with broken hearts, broken relationships, and broken, distorted images of themselves, their dreams, and their self-worth.

He's now been honored as a molder of faith and dreams in the lives of hundreds of students in Brainerd, Minnesota. At the award presentation at the White House, President Ronald Reagan read these inspiring words to him:

Teacher, you are the molder of their dreams.... You are the spark that sets aflame the poet's hand, or lights the flame of some great singer's song. You are the guardian of a million dreams. Your every smile can heal or pierce a heart. Yours are a hundred lives, a thousand lives.... Your patient words, your touch make you the god of hope. Fill their souls with dreams to make those dreams come true.

Guy divulges a secret about his teaching: Every day Guy arrives in his classroom early to sit in the seats where his students sit, and he prays for them.[11]

People often tell me they are praying for me. That always encourages me, and so I regularly pray for other dreamers to encourage them. A dream builder who prays makes a solid investment with significant rewards in a dreamer's life and dream.

FRANK BUILDS BIG

ON THE DAY THAT changed his life forever, Frank Alarcon was just a parcel-post driver in El Paso, Texas. What started as a small, simple dream of providing one decent meal for some hungry people took Frank on a journey into the miraculous. With God's help, Frank has changed lives—given a hopeful future to hundreds of the poorest of the poor in Juarez, Mexico.

On his lunch hour, Frank went, as usual, to a Bible study led by a Jesuit priest, Father Richard Thomas, in an upstairs room of the shabby building housing Our Lady's Youth Center. Father Rick read that day a passage from Luke's gospel: "When you give a banquet, invite the poor, the crippled, the lame, the blind, and you will be blessed. Although they cannot repay you, you will be repaid at the resurrection of the righteous."[12] The reading, and Father Rick's comment that he'd never really done that, set off a discussion about what might happen if the group took the passage seriously.

The poorest people he knew, Father Rick said, were the ragpickers who lived by gleaning—using and selling—the trash at the city dump in Juarez, just across the border. The imaginative group started to plan: They would prepare food in their homes and take it across the border to distribute to the ragpickers—a decent meal on Christmas Day.

On Christmas Day, about a dozen from the Bible study toted twenty-five bologna sandwiches, some burritos and tamales, fruit, candy, cookies, and a ham to the smoldering dump. The stench was unbelievable, and yet here, on Christmas Day, a few dozen people sifted through the heaps of trash. Frank's heart wrenched at the sight of one boy, about five, who sat on the ground gnawing on a melon rind.

About eleven o'clock, the Texan visitors set up a makeshift table and spread out the food. A few curious people ventured near. Father Rick said a blessing, and the ragpickers filled plates—hesitantly at first, but news traveled fast. When the first group had gone through the line, Frank climbed up to the roof of his camper to see if any more people might come share the meal. He gasped. About three hundred people, hidden from sight beyond the low hills of trash, were heading toward the table. There would never be enough food!

The group didn't panic but figured they'd keep serving until the last morsel was gone. People came. People ate and ate and, like a miracle of biblical proportions, at four o'clock the group had food left over—enough to take to two orphanages!

A bigger dream stirred in Frank's heart. One quick good deed seemed so little to give in the light of the crushing needs he'd seen that day. Frank asked God to show him what an ordinary guy, a postman, could possibly do to make a lasting difference for the ragpickers. Confident that God would continue to work in and through his dream, Frank moved across the border, into a room with a leaky roof just a few hundred yards from the dump.

> A dream builder who prays makes a solid investment with significant rewards in a dreamer's life and dream.

Because of Frank's dream—to be a dream builder for others—the lives of the dump people of Juarez have improved dramatically. Yes, they still glean the dump, but they have a staffed medical clinic, a pharmacy, a dental clinic, and a day-care center so the children have a clean, safe place to play while their parents glean. They can buy food at or below cost at The Lord's Store.

Hearing about the store, Sergio Conde Varela, an influential Juarez lawyer, came to the dump hoping to catch Frank and others breaking some tax laws. But when Sergio saw the results of Frank's work, Sergio quit his job, gave away his money, and offered to manage the store himself. Today he defends, without charge, the poor of Juarez.

Adobe homes have been built. A monopoly on recycling has been broken; the ragpickers can sell their gleanings to anyone they want, including their own recycling co-op. People who had no hope now sing a hopeful song because Frank, Sergio, the doctor, the dentist, and others stepped out in faith—took a risk—believing that they could build a dream for others.[13]

What can one person do when he or she decides to build the dreams of others? The exciting answer is that you will never know the end results of investing yourself in another dreamer, for dream building, like Don Lansing's cornfield, will multiply harvest upon harvest, year after year, in countless other lives.

NINE

Helping Children Dream

WHEN WE BECOME PARENTS, a new dimension is added to our dreams for our lives: helping our children discover and nurture their own dreams, persevere with courage when their dreams falter, and celebrate with joy when they come to fulfillment.

When Mary and I built our first house in Arizona, we wanted it to be a dream house in spite of the fact that the house itself was quite plain and simple. We talked about how much we wanted our home to be a place for our family to dream together. The day before the concrete slab was poured, we loaded our son, Patrick, and our daughter, Shawn-Marie, along with Grandma and Grandpa, into the car and drove to our new homesite. As we stood where the slab would be poured the next day, we shared our dreams about living in a new place. Before we left we placed the greatest dreamers' manual ever written, the Bible, under the prepared area as a symbol of our foundation for believing that our dreams would come true.

While we lived in that house, we often reminded one another that our home would be one place where we could each live out our dreams. Believing that it is important to create an atmosphere where we all dare to dream, we continually looked for creative ways to encourage everyone in the family to keep dreaming.

During their growing years, Patrick expressed an interest in music, and Shawn-Marie was drawn to the idea of modeling. Mary and I encouraged them to follow their dreams. We listened to sour notes as our son learned to play the guitar and piano, but as he took lessons and practiced, he improved. Today Patrick is the leader of an excellent band, The Decision, who just released their first musical compact disc.

Shawn spent time in dance and acrobatics, learning balance, poise, and other positive ways to express and present herself. She went on to win Miss Photogenic in an Arizona Top Models contest.

Helping children to begin to dream, to live out their dreams, and to experience the reality that dreams can come true enriches our lives and encourages us as well—as parents, stepparents, grandparents, aunts and uncles, teachers, and friends—to lay hold of and follow our own dreams.

CREATING THE ATMOSPHERE

"TWINKLE, TWINKLE, LITTLE STAR ..." Looking into the heavens, we can see the light of millions of magnificent stars. We can see the light of the stars only because Earth's atmosphere, which absorbs or reflects most electromagnetic radiation, has an "optical window" that allows visible light to pass through. It's this atmosphere that causes the starlight to twinkle. The atmosphere of Venus, on the other hand, allows only diffuse sunlight to pass through. The carbon dioxide, nitrous oxides, and sulphur compounds that give Venus an acid, toxic atmosphere block out the starlight. No twinkling stars there.

> As dreamers ourselves, we should encourage and support the children of our world to believe in, and live out, their dreams.

Again, Earth's particular *atmosphere* makes the stars twinkle and allows their light to shine through. Imagine for a moment that these twinkling stars represent children. What would it take to keep their light shining and illuminating the world year after year, for the rest of their lives?

It takes the proper atmosphere. Children are created to begin as, and to grow into, ever more creative and vibrant dreamers and doers. Children naturally discover new opportunities and ask bright "what ifs." But the illuminating power of their innovative, creative thinking can be dimmed or, worse yet, blocked out entirely by an acidly critical or "dense," uncaring atmosphere. Our role, then, is to create a positive, enabling, caring atmosphere that gives them a chance to shine. As dreamers ourselves, we should encourage and support the children of our world to believe in, and live out, their dreams.

Let's explore seven things we can do to help our children dream. Forgive the cute acronym TWINKLE, but for a few moments allow yourself the freedom to think of children in terms of twinkling stars. The acronym might help some readers remember these key verbs:

T   *Test* out all possibilities
W   *Work* on natural, God-given interests and strengths
I   *Involve* yourself wholeheartedly
N   *Nurture* worth and esteem
K   *Keep* balanced
L   *Lead* the way
E   *Encourage*, encourage, encourage

TEST OUT ALL POSSIBILITIES

TESTING OUT THE COUNTLESS possibilities both expands dream horizons and allows children's goals to become clearer and focused. Educators understand how important it is to nurture curiosity and to offer children many opportunities for discovery. A veteran of 40-plus years teaching kindergarten, Isabel Kresky of Lincoln Park School in Duluth, Minnesota, says, "What children learn in their first five years is almost equal to what they learn in the rest of their lives."[1]

That important early learning doesn't mean a rigorously academic preschool prep program. What best prepares children for future academic success, it turns out, "are already woven into the fabric of family life: going to the post office, taking a bath, making a meal. Merely by listening to their children's questions, encouraging their curiosity, giving scope to their imaginations, and supporting them as they explore the world, busy parents can do more than a host of preschool academic-coaching tools."[2]

And, more important than skills for academic success, what a child learns from adults are the attitudes and ways of dealing with people and situations that will frame a child's approach to life as he or she grows. Professor Herbert J. Walberg of the University of Illinois, Chicago, believes that the component of "parental attentiveness" embodied in what might be called the "curriculum of the home" makes a profound difference in how well children function in life as well as in school.[3]

In a healthy child, energy is synonymous with childhood, and that energy can be channeled for maximum benefit. Children will find outlets for their energy. Anyone who has fished an entire roll of soggy tissue from the toilet knows that it's unwise to leave a toddler unsupervised. As children grow, they still need supervision and positive direction to use their energies constructively. Experts say that *too much* involvement in *too many* activities can produce symptoms of stress in children. And yet, *no* involvement in worthwhile activities leaves children open to exploring negative or unhealthy channels for their energy.

Whatever your environment, think in terms of positive, life-expanding options. Travel, visit libraries, frequent festivals and events where children can experience other languages and cultures. Attend and participate in sporting events. Go to concerts and plays (even, and especially, the free ones offered through libraries, schools, and community centers). Tour museums.

Help children think beyond themselves. Help children see that someone's dream for a better neighborhood or world, coupled with adults' and children's actions, can have far-reaching, profound effects. You might engage their efforts and collect food for the hungry, recycle, join in neighborhood cleanups, give outgrown coats for the school clothing drive, buy a toy for the Angel Tree program. Talk with children about why you're doing what you're doing and what happens as a result.

Opening doors to possibilities doesn't need to be expensive or difficult. Reading to and with children introduces them to new worlds and allows their creativity to fill in the visual details of a story or far-away country. Activities as simple as cutting pictures from magazines to help children make their own storybooks, or making sock or paper-bag puppets, can nurture creative language and written expression. Working in the garden or on a farm, playing around with a computer, looking up at the clouds and stars, riding bicycles or riding horses, going camping or on picnics, caring for a pet, getting involved in scouts and church activities, art or music lessons, summer classes offered by community colleges . . . the list of possibilities is endless.

As the list implies, not all opportunities need to be prescheduled or prepackaged. Dr. Joseph Sparling, child development expert from the University of North Carolina, points out the value of variety in "raw materials" such as art supplies. "One sitting doesn't give a child an opportunity to discover that there are one thousand different ways to draw a house or a tree."[4]

In testing out possibilities, it is important to guard your personal desires or opinions. It's easy for pushy adults to eliminate a potentially positive experience or press an opportunity too hard. Children are tender, sensitive, and perceptive, often beyond our realizations. Our words, actions, and attitudes can either launch or ground an opportunity for a dream.

A child considering or pursuing an option can be easily intimidated by negative feedback.

> That's dumb.
> That's a waste of time.
> That's something I never got to do.
> That's too difficult or impossible.
> That's insignificant.
> That's for someone smarter or more talented than you.
> That's something you could never do.

A friend shared her own story of the power of negative feedback. She grew up in a neighborhood full of boys. One day, she was in the middle for a game of "keep away," and the boy on one side of her said to the boy on the other, "You don't have to throw the ball too high. She can't catch it anyway."

That one remark settled into her subconscious as the belief that she was incompetent when it came to sports. "I can remember being absolutely *shocked* when our junior high girls' softball coach asked me one day if I'd like to substitute for their sick pitcher. He thought *I* could pitch? Then I realized how one remark had stifled my desire to even try something I evidently had some talent for. No one had ever encouraged me that way before.

"When my nine-year-old son asked if he could join a bowling league, my first thought was that it was a big commitment of time and money. Besides, nobody else in the family bowled. But as I reflected on the effects negative attitudes had in my life, my second thought was, 'Why not, if he wants to try?' He's been on a team for several months now and he loves it. His older brother took a rock-climbing class, loves bicycling, and is scuba certified—things that make me cringe sometimes. As a result of my experience, though, I purposed never to discourage my children from learning and at least giving things a try."

A discouraging word can shut down a child's adventuresome spirit. Remember, your child's dream may be different from your own. But that's only half the story. An adult's expectations for a child can unwittingly put that child under unhealthy stress. At his parents' suggestion, Ethan, the eight-year-old son of some friends, joined the local swimming team. He was a good swimmer and enjoyed recreational swimming, but the competitive nature of the swim team just was not for him. His parents sensed this and, after a four-week trial, asked him if he wanted to stay on the team. Ethan replied that he didn't, but started to sniffle and went on, "But, Mommy, if I quit, I'll waste the money you spent on my swimming suit."

His mother quickly reassured him that, as long as he had gained something from the experience—better skills, new friends, or even the knowledge that competitive swimming wasn't for him—it wasn't a waste of time or money. "But I wondered," she recalled, "if I had unknowingly, sometime, put such emphasis on achievement and frugality that it made him afraid to even *want* to quit something he didn't enjoy. I remember wanting to do so many things that my parents wouldn't, because of time or cost, let me try. Maybe I've gone too far the other way and put pressure on my kids to stick with things that just weren't for them. I want to be sure they have the freedom to discard, as well as try, opportunities."

As I grew up, my parents continually presented options to me. In grade school, I took music lessons, acted in plays, played the trumpet, joined the basketball team, toured our nation's capital, and talked to foreign missionaries who stayed in our home. These experiences and many more helped me discover what I did and didn't like. I learned what I did best and what I did poorly. My wife and I passed this chance for discovery on to our children by making sure they had sporting, dancing, music, acting, educational, travel, mission, and church experiences.

Testing out a multitude of possibilities is part of steering children in the directions of success and significance in living out their dreams.

WORK ON NATURAL, GOD-GIVEN INTERESTS AND ABILITIES

As you open the door to a variety of options, note a child's interests, abilities, and strengths. Then share in the adventure of building a child's dreams upon those foundation stones.

I like the familiar slogan "God don't make no junk." The grammar may be poor, but the meaning is rich. God makes all children valuable. Every adult is called to be a child's gold miner. We need to dig and dig to help them find the golden nuggets of God-given gifts that can be crafted into the beautiful treasures of dreams.

What's the best way to discover and develop children's interests, abilities, and strengths? One way is through objective screening, of the sort conducted by schools through various prescribed interest and aptitude tests. These may point out potential in areas of academic, artistic, or musical ability. There are even objective tests that relate attitudes and abilities to possible occupational paths.

Perhaps a more practical evaluation on a day-to-day basis is informal, yet intentional, observation of children and their behavior. Does your child love to play with blocks or building toys? This might indicate a propensity for spatial skills and the kinds of cognitive abilities used in design, mathematics, and engineering. Verbal and relational skills show up in pretending games. Adults can observe what kinds of toys a child gravitates toward. Does the child love to doodle and paint? Is the house filled with fish, birds, and hamsters? The things that hold a child's interest can tell you much about a child's natural aptitudes.

No two children, even of the same age level or in the same family, are the same. Encouraging natural abilities and interests again requires that a parent not try to push a parental agenda. Being a child's dream builder involves paying attention to, and respecting, the child as an individual. In one family I know, music is very important to the parents. They encouraged their children to learn to play a musical instrument. One child took readily to the piano and now plays three instruments. The other child was consistently frustrated by the kind of discipline required to learn to play an instrument. After one year of lessons, both he and his parents were happy to look for some other form of expression. Here the parents relied on their observation skills. They often heard him singing around the house, and they recognized a good voice. They suggested he try the school chorus, where he discovered how much he loves to sing. These parents focused on their son's strengths. When one option seemed unsuccessful, they redirected his energies to another area, ultimately turning a potentially negative experience into something positive.

Other families can heed the lesson: By paying close and loving, but objective, attention to children, adults can suggest activities for which children might not recognize they have the talent.

There's another element in discerning a child's God-given abilities: Ask for insight from the Giver of all good gifts. Pray, asking this question: *What would I see, if I could see each child through God's eyes, not my own?* Ask God to awaken in you perception and true understanding of who our children are—their hopes, hurts, fears, strengths, and dreams.

An old folk tale illustrates the importance of working on natural, God-given abilities and strengths:

> The animals once decided to go to school. The curriculum consisted of running, swimming, flying, and climbing. It was the policy of the school administration that all the animals had to take all of the subjects.
>
> The duck excelled in swimming, but was a poor runner because of its webbed feet. The rabbit ran like a track star, but failed swimming. Everyone was amazed by how well the squirrel could climb, but they were just as amazed by how poorly the squirrel flew. And the eagle soared magnificently, but could not run, swim, or climb well at all.

Most fables have a moral, and this one is no exception. Build a child's dreams on the child's best qualities, and that child can become all that he or she was designed to be.

INVOLVE YOURSELF WHOLEHEARTEDLY

WHATEVER HIS OR HER strengths and interests, a child is rarely able to seize a dream without the wholehearted involvement of parents, stepparents, grandparents, teachers, and/or significant others. Teachers will tell you they can pick out the students whose parents take an active part in their children's lives. Involvement makes a difference.

Involvement is not control. Control is manipulative and contrived. Involvement means putting the needs of the child ahead of one's own needs. It means making what is important to the child a priority. It means being present to celebrate in victory and comfort in defeat.

Some children exhibit a strong desire or talent in a particular direction early in life. Eric is one of those. From the age of three, he said he wanted to be an astronaut. His parents acknowledged his interest and provided books on space and space construction toys, but, knowing that children's interests change over time, they also exposed him to things like swimming lessons and programs at the zoo.

By early elementary school, he still expressed the same desire, so they helped him with science fair projects and took him to summer "fun science" and math classes at the community college. But they also went camping as a family and helped with his Cub Scout activities. They encouraged him when he applied for scholarships to Space Camp in Huntsville, Alabama. When he was accepted, they made a family vacation of driving him to Alabama to attend the program. The year Eric's friend won a scholarship, but he didn't, Eric's parents expressed their pride in his attitude of being glad for his friend.

Eric's mom says, "I've given freezer space to science experiments, made pizza for all-night study sessions for the Science Olympiad team, and found a photo shop that would make five-by-seven prints in one hour for a state competition. His father helped rig a platform to simulate earthquakes for a science fair project and drove a bit out of his way every morning for several years so that Eric didn't have to spend an hour on the city bus to attend a magnet school. It became obvious to us that this was more than a passing whim; Eric was truly committed to his dream. We talked about it, and talked realistically about how he could still find satisfaction if things fell short of his big dream of becoming an astronaut."

Taking Eric's dream seriously has been a family project, and the family has helped draw Eric closer to his dream. His first two years out of high school, his summer job involved studying and mapping data from the *Magellan* Venus probe. The next summer, he was an intern at NASA's Goddard Space Flight Center. This year he looks forward to an internship with Russian scientists near Moscow.

"Sometimes it's been scary, standing with Eric in faith and telling him we believed he could realize a dream that so few people achieve. We saw that he had the abilities, and he feels God's call to use his gifts this way. We've always felt we needed to do what we could—both to honor what God has gifted him with and because we love Eric. It has taken our time, resources, and prayers, but it has all been effort well invested because of who Eric has become through pursuing his dream."

My own parents stayed involved with me and my dreams until the day they died. In school sports, I could count on seeing my dad lead the cheer when I would score a run. Mom was always in the audience smiling when I performed. They believed in my dreams and, more important, demonstrated that they believed in me by remaining wholeheartedly involved, whether I did well or did poorly. When my teachers invited my parents to school, they were there to share in every detail of my academic, emotional, physical, and relational development. I'll never forget that gift they gave me.

Involvement is an act of love. Today adults' schedules seem to be overcrowded with urgent things, and often truly important things—like helping children dream—get shoved aside. Although "helping children dream" wasn't included on their list, the findings of a survey by the PTA/Dodge National Parent Survey are discouraging. The survey indicated that parents were more likely to talk than to act. Ninety-two percent of survey respondents talked with their children about school. Seventy-three percent helped with homework, and the numbers continued to fall from there. Only 52 percent read with their child, and a mere 17 percent talked to teachers. A scant 13 percent took their child to a library.[5]

> **Involvement is an act of love.**

This lack of involvement has teachers losing patience with parents who decry their children's poor performance and demand more of schools, but fail themselves to take an active, positive role in the mental, moral, and emotional development of their children. "Judging by what they do rather than the lip service they offer, many of today's parents plainly put their own needs, and especially their careers, ahead of their children. While some of that is understandable, particularly in households where merely keeping food on the table is a dicey proposition, the unpleasant consequence is a void schools cannot fill."[6]

Dr. Nick Stinnet shares his findings after studying three thousand families.[7] He found that strong families

- Are committed to the family
- Spend time together
- Have good family communication
- Express appreciation to each other
- Have a spiritual commitment
- Are able to solve problems in a crisis

Dr. Stinnet's research seems to confirm that involvement builds strong families. Strong families provide a solid foundation for building strong, healthy dreamers.

NURTURING A CHILD'S WORTH AND ESTEEM

RELATED TO PARENTAL INVOLVEMENT is a child's sense of worth. Rose Ann Bernal, a parent actively involved at the Taos Pueblos Head Start in New Mexico, told interviewers at the Head Start Parent Involvement Institute in Washington, D.C., "When children see you involved in their education, it builds their self-esteem. They say, 'Are you going to another Head Start meeting, Mommy? Is that meeting for me?'"[8]

Gary Smalley suggests that the level of achievement a child finds in a future career, the habits the child adopts, the friends a child hangs around with, even the person that child marries, are related to the image that a child has of herself or himself.[9] In other words, children with poor self-images tend to make poor choices; children with good self-images tend to make good choices—not just in childhood, but throughout their lives. As William Wordsworth said, "The Child is the father of the Man."

This principle applies to dreaming as well. There seems to be a direct correlation between a sound sense of self-worth and esteem, and the ability to dream. Children who lack self-esteem and have a poor sense of their own worth are limited in their ability to dream— if they dare to dream at all. Children who have a good sense of their own worth and a healthy, self-esteem are more likely to dream big, bold dreams because they believe they can achieve.

If nurturing a child's self-esteem is so important, we need to discover all the practical things we can do to create a favorable atmosphere where self-esteem can grow. When their son Creed was four, Dallas businessman Richard Green and his wife set aside one night each week especially for him. With good behavior, Creed could earn the privilege of doing anything, within reason, he wanted on that night. One evening, that meant spending an entire hour at a discount store watching the fish in the tanks at the pet department. It was simple, it was inexpensive, but it communicated to Creed that *he* was of inestimable value to his family.[10]

Nurturing with Acceptance

WE CAN BEGIN TO nurture a child's self-worth and self-esteem with acceptance. Unconditional acceptance leads to self-acceptance. When children are accepted for *who they are*, rather than for what they have done, they feel more secure and confident. Marc Davidson speaks from his experience as director of Boston MatchPoint, a ministry to at-risk youth: "If a person continues to say, 'I care about you; I'm in your corner'—and not just says it but also demonstrates it— that has a compelling impact on kids. There's a *power* in unconditional love." Davidson's colleague, Scott Larsen, agrees: "Every kid needs at least one adult who believes in him, because they don't believe in themselves."[11]

If children are repeatedly told, by words or subtle attitudes, that their worth and value is based on performance, they will likely choose to do only what is "safe" and predictably achievable. They will be afraid to take risks, because risk opens the possibility of failure. And failure is perceived as a personal disaster. People who are daring dreamers have learned that the word *failure* describes an event—not a person.

Nurturing with Approval

NURTURING A CHILD'S SELF-WORTH and self-esteem requires positive approval. From infancy through maturity, all humanity craves approval. We all long to hear and know that we are okay.

Every child is valuable. In our culture, however, it is too easy to be sucked into thinking that the attractive or physically strong are more valuable than the rest. When they are young—and as they grow older—we must equip children with a knowledge of their strengths and good qualities.

Some adults believe that withholding approval will push a child to improve. Throughout my school years, I had teachers and coaches who never gave high grades or compliments. They reasoned that there is always room for improvement in anyone. That is true, but a "carrot on a stick that is continually out of reach" approach engenders discouragement rather than the incentive to strive and grow. The best motivator for improvement is honest recognition of accomplishment and approval, a "Look, this is how far you've already come, and this is where you're aiming to go" focus.

> *People who are daring dreamers have learned that the word failure describes an event—not a person.*

When we fail to provide positive approval for our children, they will pursue the negative kind of approval found through peers with nowhere dreams or by acting out unhealthy, counterproductive behaviors. This does not mean we should lend approval to everything a child does. Dr. Sal Severe, an elementary school psychologist, suggests in seminars for parents that children's negative behavior and attitudes are effectively reduced as adults consciously and consistently look for and acknowledge positive behaviors and attitudes. Along these same lines, a teacher friend noted that one of the most effective ways to calm a fidgety class is to offer approval to some well-behaved child. "Sam (or Sally), I like the way you're sitting still and paying attention." Such a statement almost always—immediately—elicits a calmer classroom, eyes on the teacher. Why? Because everyone craves approval.

It may be easy to give approval for a child who excels. It's important also to remember to acknowledge and affirm character traits and attitudes, not just abilities. This affirms who they are, rather than what they do. One child's poor performance in a game was obviously frustrating to him. On the sidelines after the game, he said to his mother, "I was so mad, but I didn't quit. I kept on trying, Mom. Didn't I? And I'm proud." His mother gave him a hug, affirming his being and approving his attitude, despite his poor performance.

Making a commitment to provide positive approval will help our children live and dream and realize what God envisions for them.

Nurturing with Appreciation

ANOTHER WAY TO NURTURE a child's self-worth is through appreciation. Experiencing love and appreciation propels children toward dreaming new dreams and envisioning new possibilities. Appreciation unlocks imagination and potential. I have a friend and partner who continually tells people, "I really appreciate you." When he says the almost magical word *appreciate*, I can see their eyes sparkle. Faces become radiant, and postures straighten. Appreciation energizes.

A man I know has saved every note of appreciation his wife has ever tucked into his lunch bag. He cherishes appreciation. So do children. Saying thank you, tucking notes or surprises under the pillow, popping out for a soda or ice cream just to say you appreciate diligence in doing homework (or for no special reason), tying a balloon to a child's chair or putting on a special plate at the table—these little everyday ways of expressing appreciation are powerful motivators and energizers.

In A.D. 399, St. Augustine noted that people travel for miles to gaze at the magnificence of the ocean. They stare in amazement at the wonders of the heavens above. They look with awe at majestic mountains. Then, without a thought, they pass by other people, God's most incredible creation. Children are magnificent creations, with dreams that can change the world. Let's tell them and show them how much we appreciate them.

KEEP BALANCED

THE NEXT KEY TO helping children dream is to help them keep their feet on the ground and their heads in the clouds. We can do this best by helping them find balance mentally, emotionally, physically, and spiritually.

Balance mentally may involve academic exercise, but it also includes having the understanding to put together, and put to practical use, facts and mental capacities. Balance emotionally addresses attitudes as well as feelings. Attitude is a choice. We need to partner positively with children to help them make the right choices and to understand why those choices are right. If children's attitudes are good, their emotional health will benefit.

It is also important to help children find a balance physically. Proper diet, exercise, healthy hygiene, and rest are all components that keep children physically balanced. Encouraging sound disciplines that help form positive habits will help build strong, healthy dreamers.

Another essential area that is part of well-balanced dreaming is spiritual stability. From the soul come the values, morals, ethics, and character that keep both the dreamer and dream on course. Without a spiritual map and compass, a dreamer can lose both direction and protection.

Even those who seem on the brink of attaining incredible dreams need a sound spiritual balance. We've seen the headlines telling of gifted athletes who became so focused on winning the gold or the championship that the goal took control. They made questionable, unethical, or plainly disastrous choices to ensure their own success, sending their lives careening out of balance.

What a contrast is Norwegian speed skater Johann Olav Koss, internationally acclaimed after setting three world records in the fifteen-hundred-meter, five-thousand-meter, and ten-thousand-meter events in the 1994 Olympic Games in Lillehammer. Joining the speed skating team at the Strommen Club near Oslo at age eight, Johann was not an apparently gifted skater, but he had a special talent for training. If the coach had to miss a skating practice, Koss would practice anyway. By the time he was twelve, Johann had already determined to aim for the dream to one day be world champion.

> *Even those who seem on the brink of attaining incredible dreams need a sound spiritual balance.*

But that wasn't his only focus. Svein Havard Sletten, his first coach, recalled that, while the other competitors paced anxiously while waiting between races at the Norwegian national championships, sixteen-year-old Johann was busy studying his English textbook. His parents wanted Johann and his two brothers to understand what life was like for the rest of the world outside of industrialized countries, so they took the boys on trips to India, Nepal, and Egypt. Johann gained new perspective on how much he and his family had together. He developed a heart that saw beyond himself to care for others.[12]

Far to the south of Norway, in Africa, young aspiring athletes—the children of war-ravaged Eritrea—knew the strength of Koss's heart. Touched by what he had seen there on a trip in conjunction with Save the Children, Johann Olav Koss promised to return after the Olympics with sports equipment for them.

Back home at the Olympics in Lillehammer, Koss focused on his dream of winning, but not to the exclusion of his dream to help the children of Eritrea. His personal donation of his bonus money—roughly $30,000 from equipment sponsors and the Norwegian Olympic Committee for winning the fifteen-hundred-meter gold medal—so challenged and inspired his countrymen, other athletes, the press, and visitors to the '94 Olympics that they donated more than $1,455,000 to Olympic Aid to aid children in Bosnia, Africa, Asia, and Latin America. Included in that total was $90,000 from Koss's auction of his own skates on the last day of the Olympics. Koss asked the children of Norway to donate their own extra, still usable soccer balls, sports equipment, and clothing; donations came in by the truckload.

Return Koss did, in a plane so filled with twelve tons of equipment that half the seats had to be removed to accommodate the cargo. When asked why he thought it was important to bring such things to people who were still in need of basic food and clothing, Koss recalled playing soccer with an Eritrean boy who had only one leg, and whose only ball was made of shirts tied together. Acknowledging the urgency of filling primary needs like shelter and food, Koss went on to say that it is all too easy to stop there without paying attention to emotional needs as well. Sports, he asserted, are an effective way to provide emotional rehabilitation from the shattering effects of war, and to give others the dignity of being seen as whole persons, rather than objects of pity.

Recognizing his great accomplishments as both an athlete and a man of great generosity, conviction, and compassion, *Sports Illustrated* named Johann Olav Koss its 1994 Sportsman of the Year. "'I've always needed something else to concentrate on besides sport,' Koss says. 'To be just involved in one thing is like standing on one leg. If you break that leg, you will fall. But if you have two legs, then you have something else to turn to.'"[13] Now retired from speed skating and busy studying medicine, Johann Olav Koss continues to pursue his dreams. He is an admirable young man who has found a balance in his life mentally, physically, emotionally, and spiritually.

Balance is an essential key to success in every arena of life. Parents hold the hands of tiny toddlers, helping them balance as they take their first steps. As children grow, adults should continue to help them find a sound balance in learning, actively living, reaching, and being, so they can step out on their own, stable and strong.

LEAD THE WAY

A MOTHER WAS WALKING along the sandy ocean shore when she noticed that her little girl was stretching her legs as far as she could to step into Mommy's footprints. The mother had a sobering thought: *If my child is following in my footsteps, I'd better be the best leader I can be for her.*

This story illustrates exactly what happens every day all over the world. Children are following where their families, teachers, or friends are leading them.

Children always pay more attention to what a person does than to what a person says. Several years ago, Zig Ziglar spoke to a group of parents at an athletic banquet. I still remember him telling us that night, "It's a kiddie-see-kiddie-do world." In his book *Raising Positive Kids in a Negative World*, he writes, "My father told me, 'Son, your children more attention pay to what you do than what you say.'"[14]

Dorothy Corkille Briggs emphasized the power of modeling when she asked, "Have you ever thought of yourself as a mirror? You are one—a psychological mirror your child uses to build his identity. And his whole life is affected by the conclusion he draws."[15]

This shouldn't be surprising. If we adults think about it and admit it, we often learn new skills more readily by watching and imitating what our "teacher" does than by listening to directions. Somehow, as adults we forget that principle when it comes to guiding children. We resort to that lame phrase, "Do as I say, not as I do."

There's a better way, modeled by trainers of Boy Scout leaders, who walk the adults through the very things they'll be teaching their young scouts. It's a "Do as I do" approach. For the adults it's an effective, though sometimes embarrassing, way to learn. It's particularly revealing and often amusing to watch adults learning to tie knots and do lashings. Learners jockey for a position close to the instructor, their eyes fastened on every move the instructor makes. Biting lips in concentration, these grown men and women call out, "Wait! Do that again! Show me again!" And, muttering under their breaths, many admit, "Now I know how the boys feel."

Would you feel confident learning to rappel from a teacher who was unwilling to join you on the cliff top, someone who merely stood at the bottom and called directions up to you? We want to learn from true leaders—people of integrity who wouldn't ask us to do anything they were unwilling to do themselves.

Our *actions* are all the more important when we consider that the average child today spends three hours a day in front of the television, and only seven minutes a day in meaningful conversation with his or her parents.[16] We have an imperative to lead with integrity and back up our words with upright and loving actions. Dr. Thomas Lickona, a contributor to *Growing Up Scared in America*, put it well: "When my father would try to teach me a lesson or discipline me, I listened because he was the same person who fixed my bike and went fishing with me."[17]

Nearly two thousand years ago, Jesus Christ said, "Follow me." His walk didn't contradict his words. The message is clear: Leading the way is the best way to bring out the greatest potential in each person, adult and child alike.

> **Leading the way is the best way to bring out the greatest potential in each person, adult and child alike.**

A *Reader's Digest* article, entitled "How to Raise a Superstar," looks at a study of 120 people who had achieved great success or fulfilled great dreams: Olympians, concert pianists, artists, outstanding scientists, and mathematicians. The research team, headed by Benjamin Bloom of the University of Chicago, identified the positive effects of parental role modeling on these "superstars." Rather than pushing to create a great talent, the parents of these great achievers "simply did what they thought was good for the child at the time." They included their children in their adult activities and avocations. They were alert to notice, promote, and reinforce signs of budding talent.

These children didn't necessarily become successful in a field of interest to their parents, yet principles were passed down from one generation to the next. A champion swimmer, for instance, remembered his father doing carpentry work. "If a section wasn't done just right, his father would tear it up and start all over again." By watching, the boy caught his father's vision and transferred it to another field of dreams. Ten years later, in a room filled with silver trophy cups and Olympic medals, he told an interviewer, "My father taught me that if a thing is worth doing, it's worth doing well."[18]

Whether teaching specific skills or positive attitudes, leading the way is the best way to help children find and dream their dreams. What's more, it's the best way to help them live their dreams.

ENCOURAGE, ENCOURAGE, ENCOURAGE

THE "E" IN *TWINKLE* may be the last letter, but it is not the least. Encouraging a child to dream is one of the most helpful things anyone can ever do.

Encouragement is like the red plate we often bring out in our home. Hand-painted white lettering on the rim of the plate reads: YOU ARE SPECIAL TODAY. Our red plate is a fun way to acknowledge and encourage each other for a job well done, an award received, on a birthday, or a "just because you are loved" day. It's a tangible way to extend honor to each other. When we use the red plate, we also go around the table, allowing each person to express words of tribute or appreciation to the one being honored.

Encouragement has a positive effect on creativity, integrity, stability, and dream-ability. Consider the following case:

A young boy wanted to earn a Boy Scout merit badge in film-making. To encourage him, his father bought Steven a super-8 movie camera. One day, the boy was inspired to make a horror movie. With a young boy's vision of what would be truly terrifying, he needed red, bloody-looking "goop" to ooze from the kitchen cabinets in one scene. His mother obligingly, and gamely, bought thirty cans of cherries, dumped the cherries into a pressure cooker, and cooked them down to a perfect state of "ooziness."

Steven's mother was a real encourager. She didn't dissuade her son. She didn't tell him to go outside and play because she didn't want all that mess in her house. Her encouragement led her aspiring son to convert her kitchen into his very own film studio. In fact, Steven's mom and dad moved furniture, made costumes, became actors in his film, and even drove to the desert in the family jeep so Steven could shoot a desert scene for his film.

Steven is, as you may have guessed, Steven Spielberg, one of the world's most talented filmmakers. Spielberg credits his parents' encouragement for helping him develop the dreams that have come true in his life.

Who can you encourage today? Encouragement should be a continual process. It is something that children, teenagers, and adults need on a daily basis. Encouragement not only helps us dream and live out our dreams—it also helps each of us become the kind of incredible person God imagined when we were born.

That growing, the journey toward becoming the person God created us to be, is the greatest dream of all for each one of us.

This simple story may be the encouragement you need to help a little one take the next step on his or her journey:

The Hand

A Thanksgiving Day editorial in the newspaper told of a school teacher who asked her class of first graders to draw a picture of something they were thankful for. She thought of how little these children from poor neighborhoods actually had to be thankful for. But she knew that most of them would draw pictures of turkeys or tables with food. The teacher was taken aback with the picture Douglas handed in . . . a simple childishly drawn hand. But whose hand? The class was captivated by the abstract image. "I think it must be the hand of God that brings us food," said one child. "A farmer," said another, "because he grows the turkeys." Finally when the others were at work, the teacher bent over Douglas's desk and asked whose hand it was. "It's your hand, Teacher," he mumbled. She recalled that frequently at recess she had taken Douglas, a scrubby, forlorn child, by the hand. She often did that with the children. But it meant so much to Douglas.

Source unknown

CONCLUSION

IT'S YOUR HAND A child is looking for to receive the affirmation, acceptance, and the assurance that he or she doesn't dream alone. It's your life that child is looking toward to model balance, perseverance, and faith. "Realize your child will be an imitator. If you have a fresh outlook on life and are willing to experiment, if you can express yourself and relate to others, if you are the fullest person you can be, you are giving your child a far greater start toward creative adulthood than could all the textbooks, methods, and creative toys."[19]

I close this challenge to provide a child with an atmosphere that promotes the reality of a shining, twinkling dream with a quote given to me and attributed to actress Josie Bisset. This truth applies to all dreamers, young and old alike.

"Dreams come a size too big so that we can grow into them."

> **It's your life that child is looking toward to model balance, perseverance, and faith.**

That growing, the journey toward becoming the person God created us to be, is the greatest dream of all for each one of us, especially for the children in our lives. They have so much potential. After all, in *their* dreams lies the future of *their* children—the future of the world.

It doesn't take a lot to help children dream and keep on dreaming. I invite you today to extend a hand to launch a dream.

TEN

Praying Your Dreams

IN PREVIOUS CHAPTERS, I'VE touched on the role of prayer in living one's dreams. But here I want to take a whole chapter to challenge you to pray your dreams. Committing your dreams to God through prayer places your dreams' responsibilities, risks, and rewards into God's hands.

Praying your dreams isn't simply mental or spiritual "magic." It is, rather, putting your complete faith in the God who believes in you and your dreams. Our dreams are meant to be God-given ideas, plans, agendas, and goals that lead to people-building and God-honoring results. Prayer gives *God-given dreamers* a *God-given drive* that prevents dreams from becoming regrets.

It took a broken neck to help Eric Lock discover how prayer puts drive into our dreams. At the age of fifteen, Eric broke his neck only thirty-three seconds into his first wrestling match. Instantly his life changed; the all-around athlete was now a quadriplegic. In the emergency room, doctors warned Eric's parents that he might not live. If he did live, doctors cautioned, he would never even breathe on his own again.

Eric and his family prayed. God answered by pulling Eric through and giving him the strength to breathe without a respirator. It's not been an easy road, but the assurance of God's presence that came from those prayers gave Eric the confidence and power to persevere and push for his physical goals. Equally important, those prayers protected Eric's spirit and kept it unbroken by the injury.

Today Eric motivates and inspires everyone around him. His dream to get up out of his wheelchair grows stronger every day.

Prayer helps Eric keep regret from replacing his dream. Eric and his family prayed—and keep praying—his dream, and God has given Eric the drive to dream beyond his limits. Prayer can do the same for you and me.

Dr. Ben Carson, a nationally known pediatric neurosurgeon at Johns Hopkins University Hospital and author of several inspiring books, acknowledges the power of prayer in his own life. "Prayer is the

> ✑
>
> **Prayer gives** *God-given dreamers* **a** *God-given drive* **that prevents dreams from becoming regrets.**

greatest power available to the individual in solving mental, physical, economic, emotional, and spiritual problems," Dr. Carson states. "Its power amazes me." He lives each day praying his dreams because he has experienced the one generating the power behind all of his dreams, as a doctor, a dad, and a dreamer.

In his book *Thinking Big*, Dr. Carson relates a riveting story about the place and power of prayer. He was operating to remove a tumor invading the brain stem of a little four-year-old girl, Christine, when suddenly the anesthesiologist yelled "Code blue!" Without warning, Christine went into cardiac arrest.

So much needed to happen instantly if they were to save Christine: turn her over, establish an airway, reestablish a normal heartbeat and circulation, administer drugs to aid her heart and help neutralize chemical imbalances in her blood brought about by cardiac arrest. Hands flew as those present put clips on Christine's skin to prepare to restart her heart. Dr. Carson thought, "'Oh no . . . we're going to lose her.' As my hands moved quickly, I was silently praying, *'Lord, I don't know what's going on or what caused this. Fix it, God, please.'*"

Dr. Carson paused for a fraction of a second before flipping Christine over, and in that moment her heart began to beat again. "'Thank you, Lord,' I said aloud. 'I don't know what happened, but clearly You fixed it.' We were able to proceed without any further difficulty. We never did figure out what had happened; perhaps it does not matter. What does matter is: I am convinced that God heard my prayer and intervened for young Christine."[1]

Dr. Carson goes on to say that, while he doesn't "count on pulling off a miracle" each time a problem arises, he does firmly believe that God cares about us in every area of life and wants us to ask for his help through prayer.

Are you skeptical about the power of prayer? Are you one of those who needs measurable proof? If so, consider this study, reported in *Maclean's* magazine. In 1988, a study on the effects of prayer tracked two groups of patients in a San Francisco hospital. One group was prayed for regularly, and the other was not. Neither group was told about the prayer (or lack of prayer). Researchers found a noticeable, positive difference in recovery in the group receiving regular prayer. On the whole, these patients spent less time in the hospital and recovered more quickly and completely than did the patients in the other group.[2] Prayer really does work wonders.

Whether you are just starting to identify your dream or celebrating your great goal, I challenge you to plug into the power of prayer. Certainly God chooses to work *through us* in working out the answers to our prayers, but it is God who makes prayer powerful. Prayer is never a waste of time.

Tiffani Fairfield and her family learned that truth through a crippling illness that has left her unable to talk. A rare neurological disorder known as Rett Syndrome has silenced seven-year-old Tiffani. Faced with such a formidable obstacle, Tiffani and her parents prayed that God would help her. Their prayers have been answered through a computer that responds to eye movements. Tiffani is able to type out messages on this computer, selecting letters by focusing her eyes on them. The computer can speak these messages aloud by means of a voice synthesizer that sounds like a young girl. What a miraculous answer to prayer! The prayers of Tiffani and her family were answered in a way they never imagined.

Surrounding your dreams with prayer gives God a chance to get involved. Earlier, I wrote, "Dream big enough to include God."

Praying about your dreams transfers the dream to God, transforms you, and transcends your limitations.

PRAYER TRANSFERS THE DREAM

PRAYER TRANSFERS MY DREAMS from my management to God's management. Dreams, by nature, contain uncertainties and can be difficult to manage. That is why I have learned to transfer the leadership of my dream's management team to God.

When I dreamed of getting a college education at Concordia College in Moorehead, Minnesota, I had big question marks about dollar signs. I didn't know how I would pay for it. Besides concerns about money, I had only average high school grades; I was uncertain whether I could survive academically. The prospect of living on my own, hundreds of miles from home, left me feeling emotionally insecure.

Once I arrived on campus, facing all these uncertainties, I made an important choice—to regularly attend a Saturday night Prayer Fellowship event, where I met other students who shared the dream of a college education. Through prayer we transferred our dreams—and our perceived obstacles—to God. Prayer provided comfort, companionship, and confidence for me as I pursued my college dream.

Dreamers travel rough roads, not well-maintained paved highways. People who live in Michigan's Upper Peninsula, where nobody even blinks at storms that deposit twenty-two inches of snow, know that an ordinary two-wheel drive automobile just isn't up to the demands of the road. Many northerners own four-wheel drive vehicles. For those who aren't mechanically minded, that means the engine's power and push is transmitted to both the front and rear axles by driveshafts. But that's not all. Because of a unit called a transfer case, the engine power can be translated one of two ways, depending on the conditions of the road. On dry, smooth roads, traditional two-wheel drive is needed. But on rough or snowy roads, the driver can shift into four-wheel drive for that extra power and control that gets you where you need to go. The driver can take advantage of the transfer case to find power to match the conditions of the road. And the wise thing for a driver to do on rough roads or in deep snow, of course, is to put the vehicle into four-wheel drive well *before* it gets stuck.

Prayer is like a transfer case for dreamers, providing the power of God that's needed for both the smoothest and even the roughest roads. Dreamers can almost count on finding setbacks along the way. By transferring their dreams to God through prayer, dreamers can find the drive they need when the road is smooth and the extra drive they'll need to turn setbacks into comebacks.

Because the road so often is rough, we should transfer our worries, as well as our dreams, to God. Though we continue to work toward our dreams, the ultimate responsibility for their fulfillment is in God's hands—and the attendant worry should be, too. Our prayers' answers depend on our God, who is dependable. Returning to that truth through prayer helps me remember to transfer my worry to God, even when the road seems impassable.

Every weekend, cars would pull into the parking lot of Community Church of Joy, only to drive away because they could find no open parking space. Those departing cars were filled with disappointed people whose needs we weren't meeting. It bothered me every Sunday to know our problem with space was turning people away. We needed more room, and the only way to do that was to relocate.

We found an orange grove that seemed the perfect piece of property, but the price tag—$3.2 million—seemed impossibly out of our reach, especially since we had only sixteen weeks in which to raise it. Faced with an impossible challenge, the leaders of our church prayed, but nothing seemed to be happening. Slowly $650,000 came in, but that wasn't anywhere near our goal.

When we saw that we were going to miss the deadline, it was tempting to worry, but we had given the dream to God; we needed to give him the worry as well. I vividly remember praying one day as I walked around the orange grove we wanted to buy. I talked to God out loud, asking him if our church was really supposed to build a new campus on the land. I listened for an answer, and what I heard in my heart gave me great peace: "Look at all these trees laden with fruit. I promise more fruitfulness from the mission that will be built here than you can see on all these thousands of trees." My eyes filled with tears and my heart exploded with joy.

I called the owner of the property and said, "I know there have been times in your life when you needed some grace. Well, Tony, our church needs your grace right now. We need more time." Without hesitation he replied, "Okay. How much time do you need?" I told him we'd need at least another month, and he agreed. Our prayer for grace was honored.

But one month stretched into two, then three, then four. In all, it took six months of working and praying, but God provided us with $3.2 million. Wow—did we throw a big party when that dream came true! What was most exhilarating, though, was what happened in all our lives. Faith became stronger. Patience grew. We drew closer to church members and friends. Unbelievable? Perhaps. Impossible? No, because, through prayer, anything is possible.

I've said that prayer works wonders. Why? Because prayer always depends on God, not on us. Even our desire to pray originates from God's deep desire to answer. We can be confident that the results of prayer—the answers—don't depend on us having the right words, but on the character of God. And God is a God who knows us, loves us, listens to us, and wants his best for us.

The effectiveness of prayer depends not on how much we know about God, but rather on how much God knows about you and me. There is nothing God does not know about us. The Bible tells us that, in fact: "Your Father knows what you need before you ask him."[3]

Later in that same chapter—the Sermon on the Mount—Jesus asks us to transfer our worry and anxiety to him.

I was a guest on the Dick Staub radio show in Chicago when an eight-year-old girl called. She said, "Every day when I go to school, I go to the monkey bars to pray. My mommy and daddy are divorced, and I pray for my dream—that we will get back together again as a family. Yesterday my brother who's three prayed with me. I like it when I can sit on the monkey bars to pray."

With a lump in my throat, I assured this little girl that God was listening to her prayers, even though her mommy and daddy couldn't stay together. In the Bible, God promises: "Before they call I will answer; while they are still speaking I will hear." [4]

Many people are afraid to pray with confidence like this little girl. They are afraid that, if the prayer isn't answered in the way they specified, their disappointment and discouragement will be too painful.

But I and thousands of others have learned that God's "no's" or "wait's" are not intended to discourage or destroy us. If this girl who called in on the radio doesn't receive the answer she is praying for, it will not be because God intends for her to be hurt. God will not abandon her or let her faith be destroyed.

Admittedly, we all like God's *yes*. God's answers, however, may be very different from what we expect. That is one reason why we become puzzled about prayer. What seems to be so right—like a mommy and daddy forgiving each other and becoming a healthy family again—doesn't always happen. The reality is that God wants all families to thrive. But God created humans as people who are free to make choices, and if people make bad choices, we cannot blame a good God. I believe God constantly looks to find encouraging ways to love and care for people like that little girl on the monkey bars. God's answers to her prayers will transcend whatever her parents decide, because God's love and power are not limited, even amid the pain and churning of life's "no's." God knows and cares for that girl's *deepest* dream—for security. And in the Psalms, God himself is called the "father to the fatherless."[5]

Knowing that God knows us that well, through prayer we can depend on God's solutions, not ours. Admittedly, sometimes God's answers to our prayers come in mysterious ways. As the Lord God told the ancient prophet:

As the heavens are higher than the earth,
so are my ways higher than your ways
and my thoughts than your thoughts.[6]

I know one man who recently learned this truth. He'd been praying about, and working toward, a vocational dream. While working overseas, he was excited to walk through doorways to a dream that God seemed to be opening for him. When he returned home filled with enthusiasm, he came face to face with the kind of personal blow that would knock to the mat most people's faith in God's goodness. His wife wanted a separation.

Confused and struggling to understand this rejection following so closely on the affirmation he sensed from God, he experienced an annoying setback: He broke a tooth. It was a minor problem, true, but frustrating, and seemingly negative. Who wants to go to the dentist? He quickly got an appointment with his wife's dentist, who happened to be a Christian. There in the dentist's chair he got to talking. While mending the tooth, the dentist directed this disillusioned dreamer to a Christian counselor experienced in marital conflicts.

In the office of a marriage counselor, this man discovered some basic principles he quickly realized were the very tools that would equip him to carry on with his dream.

What this praying dreamer initially perceived as a negative—a block—was in fact a part of God's larger *yes* for his life. In telling me his story, he confidently expressed his excitement and anticipation; he's eager to see how God will continue to answer his prayers in this unfolding life adventure.

In earlier chapters, I mentioned the importance of prayer as one faces setbacks, failures, and the loss of one's dream. I both need and want to point out here that prayer is equally important in managing success.

A story I heard about Muhammad Ali made me smile. Traveling on a plane, the heavyweight boxing champion of the world was told to fasten his seat belt. The champion laughed and said, "Superman doesn't need a seat belt." The flight attendant had the presence of mind to answer, "Superman doesn't need an airplane. Now buckle up!"

Whether the story is true or apocryphal, I don't know. But Ali was known as a man whose success had gone to his head.

I propose a better way to live in the wake of success. Through transferring our fulfilled dreams to him in prayer, God can give dreamers the balance, humility, perspective, and wisdom to accept no more than the appropriate credit, and to enjoy the rewards of success as God intended.

One of the world's most admired women, Barbara Bush, is a humble and tenderhearted, yet courageously strong, woman who frequently discusses her prayer life. Prayer is a priority for her. Prayer helps Barbara reach for the best in herself and make the most from the circumstances in her life.

In her memoirs, Mrs. Bush reveals that her husband wanted to begin his first day as president-elect by going to church. Before leaving Houston for Washington, they went together to a 7:45 A.M. service of prayer and thanksgiving. She recalls that what touched both her and Mr. Bush deeply was the prayer offered by their son George:

> Our Heavenly Father, we thank you for your many blessings. . . .
> We ask, Lord, that you open our hearts and minds to you: Many
> of us will begin a new challenge. Please give us strength to
> endure and the knowledge necessary to place our fellow man
> over self. We pray that as we face new challenges, we under-
> stand that through you we can clear our minds and seek wis-
> dom. We ask that you open our hearts and minds to prayers so
> we can feel the solace of your gentle love. Please guide us and
> guard us on our journeys—particularly watch over Dad and
> Mother. We pray that our lives be beacons to you by remem-
> bering the words of David: "May that which I speak and that
> which I have in my heart be acceptable to thee, O Lord."[7]

Through prayer, the Bush family transferred the dream of the presidency to the one who best could guide and guard the dream and the dreamer. Transferring our dreams to God in prayer transmits the power of God to us for every condition and circumstance we'll encounter.

PRAYER TRANSFORMS THE DREAM

TRANSFER LEADS TO TRANSFORMATION. Every dreamer has a picture or idea of the shape of his or her dream. By talking and thinking about our dreams together with God in prayer, we allow our dreams and ourselves to be shaped into God's ideals. Through prayer, God can take both the dream and the dreamer to a level where not just improvement, but also transformation, can take place.

Dreaming is often like building a house. The builder may start with a rough sketch and a pile of building material. Even if the builder is skilled in construction methods, without the vision of an architect and detailed blueprints, that pile of raw material is unlikely to become the lovely home it could potentially be.

I heard a story of a family eagerly anticipating the building of a new home in a subdivision. Knowing the cement slab had been poured, the husband and wife went to the site to check the progress. In pacing off the slab, envisioning which room went where, the husband noticed something wasn't right. He walked over to the contractor and said, "There shouldn't be a porch in this spot. I think you poured the slab wrong."

The contractor assured the owner that everything was okay. But the buyer insisted that someone go back and check out the plans.

Sure enough, the crew had measured off and poured the foundation for the wrong model. The crew didn't have the benefit of seeing, in intimate detail in their minds, the homeowner's vision for the home. The one who knew the plans like the back of his hand could envision the whole picture.

Throughout life, our vision for our dreams is limited. We can't foresee the changes and adjustments we'll need to make along the way, or even the final result of our dreams. Only God can see their greatest potential. It is essential, therefore, to pray throughout the dream-building process and let God lead us through every detail of the design.

When Mary and I built our home, we drove by the lot every day to check out the progress in construction. It was exciting to see the dirt moved, the footings and concrete slab poured, the piles of lumber turned into framing, the lengths of pipe and joints installed, the electrical wires connected, the roof set in place, the drywall hung, and the finishing touches completed. Prayer works in a similar way, transforming the raw material of our dreams into a beautiful reality.

But perhaps even more important than the transformation of the dream itself is the transformation prayer can work in the dreamer.

Susan was dying from non-Hodgkins lymphoma, her pain at times unbearable. Even so, Sue dreamed she would conquer the disease. Rather than panic at the word *cancer*, she decided to respond with prayer. Sue asked her friends to join her. She came to church and learned more about prayer in our College of Prayer. Sue asked her doctors, nurses, neighbors, friends, and work associates to pray for her dream of conquering cancer.

What Sue noticed first was the unexpected transformation in the lives of her family and friends. They had never taken prayer too seriously, but now when challenged by Sue, they turned to prayer and saw changes in their lives as well as hers: Hope began to take the place of despair. Pity was transformed to empathy. Grumbling turned to graciousness, and faith replaced fear. Restlessness became assurance, and sadness became joy. Anxiety was transformed into courage. Certainly tears and suffering lingered and continue to persist even today. But prayer has transformed the spirit of Sue and those who love her.

> **Prayer transforms the raw material of our dreams into a beautiful reality.**

And prayer has transformed their relationships. Formerly they seldom prayed together; now they pray for one another regularly. They have noticed a closeness that was without precedent in their lives. Learning how important family and friends are to one another, Susan assures, has transformed the illness into an avenue of beautiful blessing.

The extensive chemotherapy and radiation treatments she received gave Sue the best medical treatment doctors could provide, but Sue believes prayer was just as important in her recovery. The transformation was so amazing, in fact, that it took her doctor over a year to even use the word *remission*. Today Sue is in remission—her tests are clear—and she lives out her dream. Sue is certain that the recovery she is seeing is a direct result of prayer. She is being transformed physically, but she has been transformed within as well.

Sue is joined by millions of others around the world who have been transformed by prayer. Through prayer God can transform your dream. More important, God can transform you and help you grow toward becoming all you were created to be. On reflection, isn't becoming all that you were created to be the greatest dream of all?

PRAYER TRANSCENDS YOUR LIMITATIONS

PRAYER TRANSFORMS BECAUSE IT transcends human capacities. Praying about your dream is not directed toward yourself, merely reinforcing your own thoughts. Prayer is directed to God, who goes beyond all limitations and restrictions. A principal step in the Twelve Step program is relinquishment to, and acknowledgment of, a higher power. This higher power is not impersonal or aloof. This higher power is a God who is powerful enough to rule the world, yet intimate enough to live in our hearts.

The supernatural is not fantasy or hype or speculation; it is real. Ivy Olson was a single parent struggling to raise two children with integrity. Though the financial challenge was overwhelming, every day Ivy would pray that God would meet her family's needs. And he did. But on Thanksgiving Day, her cupboard was nearly bare. The only food in the house was three hot dogs and some bread. Instead of despairing, Ivy took her children to a local park for a hot dog picnic.

The food quickly eaten, Ivy's two children complained that they were still hungry. Ivy didn't know what to do but tell them she loved them and continue to pray.

As they walked home that afternoon, an elderly lady standing on an apartment balcony called down to them and invited them to join her for Thanksgiving dinner. Ivy accepted the offer and followed her children as they ran up the steps. Everyone enjoyed the delicious feast, and, when it was time to leave, their new friend—a pleasant grandmotherly type—gave Ivy a bag of food containers stuffed with the leftovers. After a hug of thanks, Ivy and her children returned home with full stomachs and joy-filled hearts.

The next day, Ivy and her children went back to the apartment to say thank-you again. They knocked and knocked, but no one was home. Then they ran into the building manager, who said that no one had lived in that apartment for months. No grandmother. No one.

Ivy is sure that she and her children had celebrated Thanksgiving dinner with an angel. She says there's no other explanation for the provision she received in her time of need.

My father often spoke of his encounters with the supernatural. When my dad was about sixty years old, suffering from a rare blood disease, doctors shook their heads and gave little hope that Dad would live through the night. My mother, with our family and friends, waited and prayed through that long night. My dad prayed also, and he later said that, after praying, he saw a brilliant vision of Jesus. Jesus told him, "Walther, I am going to let you live. I have some very important work for you to do." Within hours Dad's blood count returned to a functionable range, and he lived another twenty tremendous years.

> **A praying heart is a heart that trusts God to take the dream beyond human possibilities.**

Praying about and praying through your dream transcends even the dream itself. A praying heart is a heart that trusts God to take the dream beyond human possibilities to supernatural potential. Think about those times when a powerful idea unlocking the dream has come into your mind; or when a person has come into your life at the right time or place to help the dream become a reality. Prayer at work? Probably. Recall when some resource you needed for your dream to reach its fullest potential came along from a source you never expected. Prayer working again? It's sure possible.

Even the "ordinary" can be extraordinary. Chip, a friend of mine here in Phoenix, has been hoping, praying, and working to find a job and relocate back East. So far—in spite of networking and sending off hundreds of résumés—no "possibilities" have resulted in a job. When the answer to your prayer seems to be put on hold for years, it's hard to keep praying and to feel "faith-full." Regardless of his feelings, Chip kept his dream alive.

Then a few weeks ago, Chip and his wife, Rose, experienced an extraordinary "coincidence" in an otherwise ordinary day. The encounter left them certain that God is at work on their dream.

The day after Christmas, they joined the ranks of millions searching for bargains and running errands they'd put off until after the holidays. Their to-do list included "wash car." But the task proved more complicated than they expected. When they drove into the local car wash, the attendant said the equipment had broken down. They could expect about an hour's wait.

My friends left to run a few other errands and then checked back in: car wash equipment still down, still a line. So they went to one more nearby store, resigned to make the best of the delay. Finally, Chip and Rose returned to the car wash. At last, the problem was solved and the line was running. With a trunk full of packages, they decided to watch the car while it was being vacuumed. As they waited, a pickup truck pulled in right behind their car. Out stepped a former coworker of Chip's. Chip hadn't seen this man in seven years and had no idea what had become of him.

In conversation, Chip learned that this man had moved to Ann Arbor, Michigan—Chip's hometown. He owns a company. Business is booming, and he anticipates the need to hire soon. That bit of information was amazing enough to Chip, but then he found out that this man and his wife hadn't planned to come to Phoenix for Christmas. But on the spur of the moment, they had packed up the truck five days earlier and driven out to see their children.

A coincidental meeting? Chip doesn't think so. He had no idea there was any need for his specialty in his old hometown. He hadn't considered looking there for a job. He'd lost all track of this co-worker. How many variables had to work together to make such a coincidental meeting—at a car wash, of all places—possible? What were the odds this would happen strictly by chance? To Chip, that ordinary day and ordinary encounter bore the unmistakably extra-ordinary fingerprint of God.

Even though Chip still waits to see what, if anything, will come from this meeting, what he does know without a doubt is that God's hand can transcend the limits of our imagination and scope to bring our dreams into being.

PRACTICAL PRAYER POINTERS

HERE ARE SOME PRACTICAL suggestions for putting prayer into your own dreams:

1. Set aside five minutes every day to pray about your dreams. It isn't necessary to pray out loud. Simply focus on God and on your dreams, in that order. This opens your mind to receive God's insights.
2. Tell God in your own words about your dream. Talk to God like you talk to a friend. Be as specific or general, as elaborate or simple as you choose. God understands it all.
3. Pray as you live out your day. Pray in the car or on the bus or at your desk. Imagine that God is working beside you. Anywhere you may be, you can share short conversations with God—thirty-second prayers with your eyes closed to block out any distractions. The more often you do this, the more you will sense God's involvement in your life and dreams.
4. Do not always ask for something, but spend time thanking God for everything and anything: for small victories, for patience learned through setbacks, for suggestions that might help you stay on course, for a stranger's smile.
5. Pray for other people's dreams. Pray a dream-builder's prayer. Ask God to help their dreams come true. Praying for others moves us beyond ourselves.

6. Pray for the dream to be done God's way, because that's the best way. Every morning as I get out of bed, I slide down on my knees and pray my own adaptation of a hymn-prayer by Adelaide Pollard: "Have your own way, Lord. Have your own way. You are the potter. I am the clay. Mold me and make my dream after your will. While I am living this day, you will fulfill." This simple prayer may help you launch each day as well.

7. Pray for an attitude that is filled with trust in God. Trusting God with our dreams fills us with new courage and confidence.

8. Pray for healthy relationships. Relationships that are unhealthy block our creativity, imagination, innovation, and productivity. We become drained instead of inspired.

9. Pray for persistence. The single greatest reason for dream failure is giving up and quitting. Nothing significant is ever attained without perseverance. The dream's payoff comes from seeing it through, with God at your side.

10. Pray with enthusiasm and expectation. Pray as if you believe God is listening to and answering your prayers.

Are you praying your dreams today? I encourage you to stop reading and start praying, because God never stops listening or answering our prayers. The power source is available. Are you plugged in?

Dear God,

Thank you for my dreams. I give them back to you to make them all they can possibly be.

Amen.

ELEVEN

✑

Dying *for*, Not *with*, Your Dreams

IF THEY PERFORM AN autopsy on me after I die, I pray that no one will find any unfulfilled dreams left inside of me. One of the most tragic things that could possibly happen would be to die with my dreams. I am willing to die *for* my dreams, but not *with* them.

Woodrow Wilson made this observation:

> All great men and women are dreamers. Some, however, allow their dreams to die. You should nurse your dreams and protect them through bad times and tough times to the sunshine and light which always come.

Christa McAuliffe died living out her dream: to experience and to open up to young students the world of space travel. When chosen to be a crew member of the space shuttle *Challenger*, Christa was thrilled. Preparing for the voyage was a dream come true. She was aware of the dangers and risks—but willing to give her dream a chance. Tragedy struck when the *Challenger* exploded seconds after launch. Yet those who died—Dick Scobee, Michael Smith, Judy Resnick, Ellison Onizuka, Ron McNair, Greg Jarvis, and Christa— did not die with their dreams still inside. They died for their dreams.

So great was their belief in the dream that June Scobee, wife of Commander Dick Scobee, aided by the families of the other astronauts, founded a center to continue to educate and motivate children to understand and embrace the dream of space exploration.

Now expanded to include centers in several cities, The Challenger Center for Space Science Education is not simply a memorial to those who lost their lives pursuing their dream but a living investment of their dream in the lives of thousands of children. *The Dream Is Alive*, says the title of a popular IMAX film. The dream of the *Challenger* crew is truly alive.

> **A full life is a "dream-full-filled" life.**

I am not suggesting that dreamers become reckless or that dreamers purposely endanger themselves. The important principle is that we all live so fully that we are living out the dreams God planted in us when we were born. Jesus said: "I have come that they may have life, and have it to the *full*."[1]

A full life is a "dream-full-filled" life. Reinhold Niebuhr, a respected theologian, emphasized that dreaming creatively is even better than being learned. Creative dreaming is the true essence of life. Henry Wadsworth Longfellow urged people to be walking dreams.

Oswald Chambers, in his benchmark book on the Christian walk, said,

> The only way to be obedient to the heavenly vision is to give *our utmost for God's highest*, and this can only be done by continually and resolutely recalling the vision. The test is the sixty seconds of every minute, and the sixty minutes of every hour."[2]

GIVING THE UTMOST

In high school, I sang "Climb Every Mountain" for our senior banquet. This familiar—and admittedly sentimental—song has always held a special meaning for me. As I've tried to live out my dream, I've often reflected on these lyrics: "Climb every mountain, ford every stream." The song speaks of giving one's all to a dream and in the end finding joy.

Climb every mountain

EVERY GREAT DREAM IS worth the climb. Paul Petzoldt, the man others have called "the father of wilderness education," made his first ascent of Wyoming's Grand Teton in July 1924, wearing cowboy boots and equipped with a pocket knife to cut footholds in the ice. Unprepared as they were, it took Paul and his climbing companion two attempts to reach the summit and to change the direction of Paul's life.

Over the next seventy years, Paul climbed the Tetons again and again as a climber and as a guide, founded the Petzoldt-Exum School of American Mountaineering, trained American ski troops during World War II, and helped establish the first American Outward Bound school. He began the National Outdoor Leadership School in Wyoming and the Wilderness Education Association, organized to promote professionalism in outdoor leadership.[3]

Paul has spent a lifetime learning and teaching others to push back the boundaries of their limitations and venture into the wilderness with the wisdom to keep themselves and the wilderness unharmed. At the age of eighty-six, nearly blind, Paul made his seventieth anniversary climb of the Grand Teton, encouraging and instructing the novices in the party. Paul has, literally, kept climbing.

And Paul Petzoldt would be the first to tell you that climbing the mountains that rise before you takes knowledge and planning, flexibility and commitment. Climbers literally must "know the ropes" that can mean the difference between a successful climb and a disastrous fall.

And dreamers can learn something from mountain climbers. Robert Schuller wrote a book, *Tough Times Never Last—Tough People Do*. That phrase is appropriate for dreamers. Every great dream involves tough climbing, but every great dream outlasts the tough climb. Great dreamers study the mountains that rise before them, planning alternate routes and looking for footholds of opportunity in the very "rock" of problems to help them keep moving forward. Great dreamers use opposing forces to help maintain their balance. Knowing that an "easy rescue" is probably not an option, they focus their energy on achieving what they have set out to dream and do.

Cherrill Satterfield's great dream faced a whole range of mountains. Cherrill needed a liver transplant. Because she earned a few dollars more than the state-funded health care system allowed, and because of her age, Cherrill was told she didn't qualify for any medical assistance. Caught in a crack in the medical system, Cherrill's dream seemed unreachable, and eventually her health deteriorated so much that doctors questioned her chance of survival, even with an immediate transplant.

But Cherrill looked for footholds. Recognizing that this wasn't just a problem for her alone, but for many other working people who couldn't qualify for the assistance, Cherrill knocked on door after door at the state legislature. She went on local radio stations and talked to newspaper reporters. She enlisted the prayers and support of ordinary citizens in a letter-writing campaign. She used every ounce of what strength she had to keep on climbing until Arizona's Governor Fyfe Symington and the legislature changed the law. Cherrill's own health-maintenance program reevaluated her case and deemed her eligible.

> **Every great dream involves tough climbing, but every great dream outlasts the tough climb.**

After facing surgery to repair a damaged artery to her liver, in July 1995, Cherrill received her new liver. But transplant surgery is a mountain in itself, especially considering Cherrill's fragile condition. When she showed increasing signs of rejection, Cherrill's doctors performed an additional surgical procedure. Cherrill has not found sudden, miraculous improvement since her surgery. She continues to improve slowly. Up and over every mountain of this lofty range, Cherrill's faith keeps her climbing.

Ford every stream

A NARROW OR SHALLOW stream can be crossed with a short jump or a few quick steps on convenient stones. But not every stream is so easily forded. Recently my son, Patrick, and his wife, Shannon, joined me for a hike into Oak Creek Canyon, where we faced some formidable streams. Every place where the trail crossed the creek we had a choice to get across the water or turn around and go back home. Fortunately, we "moved on out" and saw incredible sights as a result. Standing still or turning back would have robbed us of beauty beyond description.

Crossing a stream safely, a backpacking guide suggests, begins before you even set foot on the trail: Study the route on a topographical map to bypass potential problem crossings and to look for headwaters, meanders, and mild grades where water will flow more slowly. Then pause at a good vantage point to assess the stream and look for narrows, bends, and waterfalls that you might not be able to see from stream level.

Great dreamers know that swift forces and circumstances and situations can spring up that could sweep them away from their dreams. We generally don't have the luxury of a "map" charted by people who have gone before us to show us the way to our dreams. But we can gain a good vantage point if we ask God to give us wisdom and vision when we encounter problems that would carry us away from our dreams.

The hiking guide goes on with tips: Streams in forested areas can conceal submerged trees on which a hiker can trip or wedge a foot. Similarly, in a dangerous "forest," dreamers can get wedged by hazards such as misunderstanding and criticism. Look for the secure footing of God's guidance, like a solid rock or a tree spanning the stream. Look for the clear water of the truth, about yourself and your dream, to keep from being trapped in the stream. If you do fall into "white water," point your feet downstream until you come to a spot where you can swim for shore; point yourself in God's direction and trust God to carry you to a place where you can safely stand.

When hiking with others, the guide suggests, one person should, if possible, stand in the stream to help pass packs across and to "spot" the other crossers. And then there's the issue of equipment: footwear and a walking stick or ski pole. The guide concludes by recommending crossing as a team, having an emergency plan, and trusting your instincts.

Who would think so much is involved in safely fording a stream? For dreamers, a "swift-flowing stream" can sweep you off your feet, dousing you, drowning you, or carrying you away from the path of your dream. But a stream does not have to be an impassable barrier. Bringing wisdom and good judgment to bear, and entrusting the outcome to God, can help you safely cross and continue your dream's journey.

Some great words for a dreamer to remember are found in the Bible:

> If any of you lacks wisdom, he should ask God, who gives generously to all without finding fault, and it will be given to him. But when he asks, he must believe and not doubt, because he who doubts is like a wave of the sea, blown and tossed by the wind.[4]

Asking God for wisdom lifts us above "stream level" to see beyond the immediate struggle and to perceive "submerged" dangers and points where we might safely "cross." Trusting in the wisdom God gives us, through the Bible or through sound counsel or the advice of dream mates, is like planting your pole solidly in the stream. With God and a dream mate, we have three solid contact points. Even in deep waters, we can face the stream and move across.

It's always wise to hand your burdens, like a hiker's pack, to God before you set foot in the water. Then you won't be pinned under the weight of your cares and concerns if you lose your footing. Ultimately, what we as dreamers have to depend on in negotiating the forces and circumstances that would cause us to falter is God's presence in the water with us and his promise:

> "When you pass through the waters, I will be with you; and when you pass through the rivers, they will not sweep over you. . . . For I am the LORD, your God."[5]

SUMMARIZING THE DREAM LAUNCH

WE'VE COVERED A LOT of ground in this book. Let's clearly enumerate practical points for taking your dream from the idea stage to its launch and realization. Consider these steps:

Start at the finish line

LIVE "AS IF" THE dream had already come true. Fulfilled dreams always work backwards. In chapter 1, I mentioned that I came to Community Church of Joy with a dream. Yes, at the time the church had only a handful of members and a small budget—barely enough to pay my salary. But I dreamed of a church that offered something for everyone in the family.

One of the first important things I did was to write out as specifically as possible what everything would look like ten years from the day I began. I dreamed of a church that would attract people who didn't go to church. In ten years, I projected, we would be meeting the needs of three thousand members, with a budget for the mission of one million dollars. Starting at the finish line helped me *begin living* my life as a leader of three thousand people, not two hundred. The changes that had to be made with the church's leadership and structure were an important part of carrying out the dream as well. The more actualized the dream is in the beginning, the stronger the dream grows. Today, over 60 percent of the twelve thousand constituents who call Community Church of Joy their church are people who previously didn't go to church. My dream to build a church for the unchurched is actually coming true.

Sharpen the dream's purpose

A RECENT SPEAKING ENGAGEMENT took me to Virginia. My host drove me to the top of a ledge on the Blue Ridge Mountains. Unfortunately, it was a hazy day so I had to choose to believe my host's superlative description of the scene on a clear day. The haze prevented me from seeing the beauty that was there.

Great dreams are magnificent. That is why it is essential to remove any haze that obscures your dream's purpose. Sharpen your dream's purpose by asking key questions:

WHY—is my dream important?
WHO—will my dream benefit most?
HOW—is my dream going to come true?
WHERE—is my dream going?
WHAT—is most important about my dream?
WHEN—will my dream be successful?

It is a good idea to revisit these questions at the beginning of each new week. Dream purposes can easily grow fuzzy. Keeping your dream purpose sharp will keep it on course.

Share the dream's possibilities

SHARE YOUR DREAM WITH as many people as you possibly can. In sharing your dream possibilities with other people, you generate interest, you receive input, and you commit yourself publicly to your dream. The accountability that comes with sharing your dream can help keep you on course when you might otherwise be tempted—by doubts, fears, or weariness—to turn back or veer away from your dream.

Sharing your dream can bring you encouragement in those times when you feel you're standing alone. Sharing your dream helps develop a dream network that leads you to needed resources, to encourage other dreamers, and to make the dream seem more real.

It can be dangerous to share your dream. There are dream discouragers with dispiriting words lying in the weeds all around us. But the benefits of sharing your dream far exceed the risks.

The more I shared my dream for Community Church of Joy, the more it grew. Along the way I discovered that sharing a dream brings more people to share *in* the dream.

Surround yourself with a dynamic dream

AS AMERICA PREPARES FOR each Summer Olympics, there is a great deal of excitement about the "Dream Team"—a team composed of the best basketball players in the world. Those players share the dream of working together to win the gold medal. To launch your dream, surround yourself with a dynamic dream team.

My mother constantly reminded me how important it was to choose good friends. My friends' influence on me would either make me a stronger or a weaker person; they would affect my attitude as well as my actions. Mom was right. The friends I chose would influence me positively or negatively.

I remembered the lessons I learned from her when it came time to hire a church staff. I looked for people who knew how to develop and maintain healthy relationships. People were the bottom line. Carl Einstein of *Success* magazine states that 87 percent of all people who fail are very capable but not very compatible. Their problem is relational, not professional. I looked for positive relational qualities—people with a positive faith, good listening skills, a sense of humor, a friendly personality, a tender heart, and a willingness to dare to dream big.

Second, I looked for people who were committed to being a lifetime learner. People who resolve to grow until they go will not become obsolete or out of touch. They must be willing to grow mentally, emotionally, physically, and spiritually.

I continue to surround myself with people—friends and work associates—who model perseverance, patience, and kindness. They don't have to be the most talented, but they do have to be positive and loving. I go for character and conviction over credentials. Launching a dream requires surrounding yourself with a dynamic dream team.

Study the dream's vital signs

OUR VITAL SIGNS ARE the first things a doctor checks when we go for a checkup. If our heart rate is abnormal or our blood pressure high or if we have a fever, the doctor will investigate to find out why. For our dreams to be successful, they need to be healthy, and we as dreamers need to remain healthy. I'm not just talking about physical health. Good health includes every dimension of the dream and the dreamer.

Total Quality Management emphasizes the importance of check-ups. A cycle of continuous quality improvement includes:

PLAN
ACT
DO
CHECK

This cycle of quality corrects errors and avoids breakdowns. Dreams need continual adjustment to keep them on course and avoid destruction.

PLAN DREAM
ACT ON DREAM'S IMPROVEMENT
DO DREAM
CHECK DREAM

I am always studying my dream's vital signs. I welcome feedback, input, evaluations, and critiques. Dreams are too important not to keep a finger on their pulse.

Stay energetic

LAUNCHING AND SUSTAINING A dream takes enormous energy. Becoming and staying energized is essential if your dream is to come true. We become energized by plugging in to the power of God, welcoming him into the dream and the dreamer. We stay energized through regular prayer—daily conversation with God—and meditation.

General Norman Schwartzkopf revealed that, in the heat of the Desert Storm conflict with Iraq, he put his hand in God's hand to give him the strength and power he needed. That was how he stayed energized through Desert Storm, and every dreamer with a dream can, and needs to, do the same.

> We stay energized through regular prayer—daily conversation with God—and meditation.

Physical activity also energizes. I exercise regularly to stay in shape and be fit to meet the rigors of my dreams. Dreams need all the energy we can put into them.

Savor the dream delights

AMID ALL THE CHALLENGES of launching a dream, it is often too easy to miss the delight. I have paraphrased an engaging commentary that can help every dreamer savor dream delights:

> While launching your dream,
> relax, limber up and be sillier,
> take fun trips and act crazier,
> climb more mountains, swim more rivers,
> and watch more sunsets,
> do more walking and looking,
> eat more ice cream and less beans,
> travel lighter and further than you've gone before,
> start barefooted earlier in the spring and
> stay that way later in the fall,
> laugh more and play hooky more,
> ride more merry-go-rounds,
> and pick more daisies.[6]

LIVING YOUR DREAM

DELIGHTING IN YOUR DREAM prepares you to live that dream.

Life at its greatest is living your dreams. Many people spend a lifetime planning or preparing to live or dreaming of living, but they never *live* their dreams. What holds people back? The answer is simple: themselves. That's right. Time and again I see people holding back as they watch other people live their dreams.

A fourth-grade teacher was not willing to accept "holding back" from any of her students. One day, she asked her students to write down everything they could not do. The papers she collected were filled with "I can'ts." What did she do with them? She put the papers in a shoe box, tucked it under her arm, and led her class to the school yard, where she proceeded to dig a deep hole. Placing the box in the freshly dug "grave," she buried the "I can'ts" forever. To celebrate the "death" of all the "I can'ts," the children had a party. And after that day, whenever a student said, "I can't," the teacher retorted, "'I can't' is no longer living."[7]

Are your "I can'ts" dead? Now would be a good time to write them down, go outside, dig a hole, and bury them. Then come back inside, throw a big party, and celebrate your new life living your dreams.

LOVING YOUR DREAMS

IT IS EASIER TO live your dream when you love your dream. I smiled at the punch line of a television commercial during the NBA play-offs: "I love this game." It wasn't hard to join in the spirit of the commercial—pumped full of energy, action, vitality, and fun—and say "YES!" myself.

I can say the same thing about my dream: "I love this dream!" I love the drama, demands, and destiny of the dream. As in relationships, loving your dream is a choice, an action, an act of your will. When you love someone, you give that person value and respect. When you love your dream, you give it greater value and respect. You are more passionate about it. You become more committed to it. To me, a dream represents something bigger than myself. Dreams are the doorway to a dynamic life.

You may have forgotten your high school physics lessons, but let me remind you about "statics and dynamics": *Static* means that which is at rest, dormant, stationary, neither active, moving, nor changing. Surely you've felt the "zap" that comes from walking across a deep rug on a cold, dry day. Or as a child you rubbed your hair with a balloon so your hair would stand up straight from your head. These are examples of static electricity—a charge that remains on an object but doesn't "go" anywhere. Then there's dynamic electricity. *Dynamic*, from the Greek word for *power*, *dynamis*, refers to forces in motion, forces producing or governing movement or activity.

Current (or dynamic) electricity gets things done. *Dynamo* is another name for a generator—in physical terms, a machine that transforms mechanical energy into electrical energy; in terms of human beings, a dynamo converts ideas into powerful action.

> When you love your dream, you give it greater value and respect.

Andrew Singleton's parents had an idea. Though Andy had an IQ of 55, indicating that he was intellectually challenged, his mother and father chose to believe Andy could and should somehow know the "ordinary" joys average teenagers take for granted as part of growing up—things like going to a regular high school. The Singletons converted their hopes for Andy into action.

Though Andrew spent most of his growing years in special-needs centers, in 1992, when Andy was nineteen, his parents enrolled him in a special class for the intellectually challenged at Middletown High School in Newport, Rhode Island. Andrew faced a lot of pressure trying to adjust, and his mother and father knew that it was expecting a lot for his peers to understand him and his struggles. Still, they held onto the dream that Andy would be accepted and would establish some friendships. They supported his efforts, and gradually that idea took on substance as Andy made good friends. Andy slowly grew personally—amazingly—to the point where he could even attend some mainstream classes.

On graduation day, the Singletons watched classmates shake Andy's hand and express their appreciation. Then the unbelievable happened. As Andrew's name was announced to receive his diploma, the arena erupted in thunderous applause. All 192 classmates rose to their feet, and soon the entire crowd of one thousand stood to applaud. Then his fellow students began cheering for Andrew, calling out his name. It was a day to celebrate great dreamers with a dynamic dream. The dream God had planted in his parents' hearts had transformed other lives besides Andy's. That day, the realization of that dream generated a high-voltage celebration in hundreds of hearts.

Dreams and dreamers deserve cheers and celebration. The Bible assures us that God delights in the praises of his people. When we celebrate our dreams, even God's heart fills with joy.

YOUR INVITATION TO DREAM

THIS IS YOUR INVITATION to wake up your dreams. Great dreaming is not putting your head in the clouds. Putting your head in the clouds merely obscures your view of the world and produces no positive results. Great dreaming, rather, is more like cloud seeding. Meteorologists study the clouds and actively seek ways to bring the positive good of the clouds—rain—down to the earth. Cloud seeding involves planting in the clouds the tiny, solid particles—things like dry ice or silver iodide—that encourage raindrop formation and bring the life-giving potential of the clouds to the earth to foster growth and renew life. Vision, imagination, creativity, and action are practical particles that great dreamers loft into their dreams. Around these, the life-giving potential of effective solutions, innovation, and positive change can form, fostering growth and renewing life.

Keeping our dream senses alive to the possible may mean examining things upside down and inside out, turning the kaleidoscope in the light of God's truth rather than holding it fixed in what passes as conventional wisdom. If that is what it takes, then that is what we need to do.

Open your eyes to possibility. One day, Helen Keller struck up a conversation with a friend who had just returned from a long walk in the woods. When Helen asked her what she had observed, the friend answered, "Nothing, really." Helen wondered how anyone could walk in the woods for an hour and not notice anything special. Helen thought how she, though blind and deaf, could feel the textures of the trees, smell the fragrance of the flowers, and imagine the forest around her; she marveled that her friend, though gifted with sight and hearing and other senses, could not. Helen Keller's life was an inspiration and a challenge to everyone to fully perceive the possibilities that life offers all around us.

God's intention for you—for everyone—is that you not miss even the smallest possibility that could be the seed for a raindrop, that could bring renewal and growth to you and to lives around you as you look for, and live out, God-inspired dreams.

Are you willing to seed the clouds for your dream? My highest hopes and prayers are that you will not hesitate—that you will at this very moment begin to, or continue to, pursue the dreams God gives you.

GO—AND DREAM WITH ENTHUSIASM!

Dreamer's Daily Power Thoughts from the Bible

DAY ONE

Commit to the Lord whatever you do, and your plans will succeed. Proverbs 16:3

DAY TWO

"For I know the plans I have for you," declares the Lord, "plans to prosper you and not to harm you, plans to give you hope and a future." Jeremiah 29:11

DAY THREE

This is the day the Lord has made; let us rejoice and be glad in it. Psalm 118:24

DAY FOUR

"And afterward, I will pour out my Spirit on all people. Your sons and daughters will prophesy, your old men will dream dreams, your young men will see visions. Even on my servants, both men and women, I will pour out my Spirit in those days." Joel 2:28–29

DAY FIVE

"'If you can?'" said Jesus. "Everything is possible for him who believes." Mark 9:23

DAY SIX

No eye has seen, no ear has heard, no mind has conceived what God has prepared for those who love him. 1 Corinthians 2:9

DAY SEVEN

Whatever is true, whatever is noble, whatever is right, whatever is pure, whatever is lovely, whatever is admirable—if anything is excellent or praiseworthy—think about such things. Philippians 4:8

NOTES

Chapter One: Nothing Is Impossible for Those Who Dream

1. Lynne Cherry, *A River Runs Wild* (San Diego: Harcourt Brace Jovanovich, 1992).

2. Mark 9:41.

Chapter Two: Twenty-Twenty Dreaming

1. Jack Canfield and Mark Victor Hansen, *Chicken Soup for the Soul* (Deerfield Beach, Fla.: Health Communications, 1993), 235–36.

2. Keith Miller, *Ten Minute Magic* (New York: Cadell & Davies, 1994), 40–41.

3. Genesis 1:28.

4. "Habitat for Humanity Pushed for Policy Model," *Christian Century* (April 28, 1993), 448.

5. Psalm 139:13–14.

6. Ephesians 2:10.

7. Albert Bandura, Ph.D., "Younger All Over," *Prevention* (June 1995), 66.

8. Abraham Lincoln, quoted in *Quests and Conquests*, compiled by Dean C. Dutton (Guthrie, Okla.: Life Service Publishing, 1953), 227.

9. 2 Samuel 22:31.

10. Hebrews 13:8.

11. Charles R. Swindoll, *The Quest for Character* (Portland, Ore.: Multnomah, 1987), 162–63.

12. Russell O'Quinn, "Live to the Limit: A Top Test Pilot's Story" (Kansas City, Mo.: Stonecroft, Inc., 1994.)

13. Mark 10:27.

14. Matthew 22:37–39.

Chapter Three: Everybody Needs a Dream Mate

1. Pat Riley, *The Winner Within* (New York: Putnam, 1993), 40–41.

2. Ibid., 44–45.

3. Patricia Sellers, "So You Fail. Now Bounce Back," *Fortune* (May 1, 1995), 64.

4. Dr. Sidney B. Simon, *Getting Unstuck—Breaking Through Your Barriers to Change* (New York: Warner Books, 1988), 201.

5. Dobie Holland, "Athletes for Abstinence Promotes Sexual Purity for Teens Until Marriage," *Jet* (January 10, 1993), 50.

6. Susan Reed, "Boot Camp and Candy," *People Weekly* (September 4, 1995), 87.

Chapter Four: The Dynamic Dream Equation

1. James Earl Jones, "How I Found My Voice," *Guideposts* (November 1993), 2–5.

2. William Plummer, "Mother of Them All: Carol Porter Feeds Poor Kids in Houston—Without a Cent From the Government," *People Weekly* (March 20, 1995), 87.

3. Jimmy Carter and Wesley J. Pippert, *The Spiritual Journey of Jimmy Carter* (New York: Macmillan, 1978), 216.

4. Emrika Padus with Sharon Stocker, "Hostility, Hopelessness, and the Heart," *Prevention* (February 1994), 121.

5. Daniel Goleman, *Emotional Intelligence* (New York: Bantam Books, 1995), 177.

6. Joshua 3:7–17.

7. Wally Amos and Gregory Amos, *The Power in You* (New York: Donald Fine, 1988), 173.

8. Matthew 7:7.

9. Jack Canfield and Mark Hansen, *The Aladdin Factor* (New York: Berkley Books, 1995).

10. Claire Safran, "The Winners: Women Who Beat the Odds," *Ladies' Home Journal* (May 1994), 215.

Chapter Five: Negotiating Your Dream Danger Zones

1. David G. Meyers, "The Road to Happiness," *Psychology Today* (July–August 1994), 36.

2. Proverbs 27:17.

3. Ecclesiastes 4:12.

4. Pat Riley, *The Winner Within* (New York: Putnam, 1993), 39–40.

5. M. Scott Peck, *Further Down the Road Less Traveled* (New York: Simon & Schuster, 1993), 23.

6. Don Shula and Ken Blanchard, *Everyone's a Coach* (Grand Rapids: Zondervan, 1995), 25.

7. J. Kelly Beatty, "They Touch the Future," *Parade Magazine* (July 16, 1995), 4–5.

8. Quoted in Peter McWilliams, *Life 101* (Los Angeles: Prelude Press, 1990), 170.

9. Psalm 27:1.

10. 2 Timothy 1:7.

11. Robert Frost, *New Enlarged Pocket Anthology of Robert Frost's Poems*, ed. Louis Untermeyer (New York: Simon & Schuster, 1946), 223.

12. Quoted in Daniel Goleman, *Emotional Intelligence* (New York: Bantam Books, 1995), 86.

13. Paul Schwartz, "Field of Fantasy," *Worldwide Challenge* (May–June 1994), 18.

14. Robert Schuller, *Power Thoughts for Power Living* (New York: Harper-Collins, 1993), 203–4.

Chapter Six: Renewing the Dreamer and the Dream

1. James Burke, *Connections* (Boston: Little, Brown, 1978), 1.

2. Hebrews 12:1.

3. Philippians 4:8.

4. Romans 8:28.

5. Jeremiah 31:23, 25.

6. Matthew 11:28–30.

7. Hebrews 12:1–2.

8. Roger von Oech, *A Whack on the Side of the Head* (New York: Warner Books, 1983), 9.

9. Robert Peterson, "The Wonder Workers," *Boys' Life* (August 1995), 30.

10. *Funk & Wagnall's Standard College Dictionary* (New York: Funk & Wagnall's, 1966), 645.

11. Psalm 130:7.

12. Isaiah 40:28–31.

13. Hebrews 11:1.

14. 1 Corinthians 13:4–8a.

15. M. Scott Peck, "The Rabbit's Gift," quoted in Jack Canfield and Mark Victor Hansen, *Chicken Soup for the Soul II* (Deerfield Beach, Fla.: Health Communications, 1994), 56–59.

16. Marvin Olasky, "Reneighboring the 'Hood," *World* (November 14, 1992), 10–11.

17. Kenneth Labich, "New Hope for the Inner City," *Fortune* (September 6, 1993), 84–86.

Chapter Seven: Rekindling a Lost Dream

1. Genesis 37:19–20.

2. Wally Amos with Camilla Denton, *Man With No Name Turns Lemons into Lemonade* (Lower Lakes, Calif.: Aslan Publishing, 1994), 147.

3. Caroline Wheal, "The Greatest Adventure of All," *Calypso Log* (June 1995), 16.

4. Erik Olesen, "Mastering the Secrets of Change," *Success* (October 1993), 44.

5. Philippians 1:6.

6. Philippians 2:13.

7. Matthew 17:20–21.

8. Romans 5:3–5.

9. Patricia Sellers, "So You Fail. Now Bounce Back," *Fortune* (1 May, 1995), 61–62.

10. Ray Kroc with Robert Anderson, *Grinding It Out: The Making of McDonald's* (New York: St. Martin's Press, 1987), 106.

Chapter Eight: The Art of Dream Building

1. Jack Canfield and Mark Victor Hansen, *Chicken Soup for the Soul* (Deerfield Beach, Fla.: Health Communications, 1994), 204–6.

2. Marc Lerner, "His Gift of the Future," *Reader's Digest* (June 1995), 137–42.

3. Peter McWilliams, *Life 101* (Los Angeles: Prelude Press, 1990), 251.

4. Mark 6:54–56.

5. John 14:12–14.

6. Jimmy Johnson, *Turning the Thing Around* (New York: Hyperion Books, 1993): quoted in *Parade Magazine* (August 15, 1993), 5.

7. Glen Allen, "Cautionary Tales," *Maclean's* (July 5, 1993), 57.

8. Alan Jay Lerner and Frederick Loewe, *My Fair Lady* (New York: Signet, 1956), 118.

9. Ephesians 4:29.

10. Angeles Arrien, from a speech at the 1991 Organizational Development Network, based on the work of Milton Olson.

11. Guy Doud, *Molder of Dreams* (Colorado Springs: Focus on the Family, 1993), videocassette.

12. Luke 14:13–14.

13. Frank Alarcon, "Christmas With the Ragpickers," *Guideposts* (December 1994), 2–5.

Chapter Nine: Helping Children Dream

1. Noam Levy, "Head Start Gives Youngsters the Boost They Need to Succeed," *Knight-Ridder/Tribune News Service* (March 1, 1995).

2. Kathleen Cushman, "Off to a Great Start!" *Parent's Magazine* (October 1992), 122–23.

3. Ibid, 124.

4. Quoted in Evelyn Bence, "Growing Creative Kids," *Today's Christian Woman* (July–August 1985), 83.

5. Sidebar, reported in a *Newsweek* special issue (Fall/Winter 1990), 61.

6. John McCormick, "Where Are the Parents?" *Newsweek* special issue (Fall/Winter 1990), 54.

7. Nick Stinnet, "Six Qualities That Make Families Strong," in *Family Building: Six Qualities of a Strong Family*, ed. Dr. George Rekers (Ventura, Calif.: Regal Books, 1985), 38.

8. Rose Ann Bernal, "Another Head-Start Parent Tells Her Story," *Children Today* (Winter/Spring 1993), 33.

9. Gary Smalley and John Trent, *The Gift of Honor* (Nashville: Thomas Nelson, 1987), 15.

10. Zig Ziglar, *Raising Positive Kids in a Negative World* (Nashville: Thomas Nelson, 1982), 83.

11. Quoted in Becky Beane, "But Will You Love Me Tomorrow?" *Jubilee* (Winter 1996), 10.

12. E. M. Swift, "Giving His All," *Sports Illustrated* (December 19, 1994), 84.

13. Ibid, 86.

14. Ziglar, *Raising Positive Kids*, 80.

15. Dorothy Corkille Briggs, *Your Child's Self-Esteem* (Garden City, N.J.: Doubleday/Dolphin Books, 1975), 9.

16. Josh McDowell, *Right From Wrong* (Dallas: Word, 1994), 35.

17. Quoted in Becky Beane, "Children of Violence," *Jubilee* (Winter 1996), 14.

18. Claire Safran, "How to Raise a Superstar," *Reader's Digest* (January 1995): quoted in Zig Ziglar, *Raising Positive Kids*, 75–78.

19. Marlene LeFever, *Growing Creative Children* (Wheaton, Ill.: Tyndale, 1981): quoted in "Creative Principles," *Today's Christian Woman* (July–August 1985), 78.

Chapter Ten: Praying Your Dreams

1. Ben Carson, M.D., *Think Big* (Grand Rapids: Zondervan, 1992), 231–32.

2. Susan Doyle Driedger, "Prayer Power: Can Patients Be Cured by the Faith of Other People?" *Maclean's* (September 15, 1995), 42.

3. Matthew 6:8.

4. Isaiah 65:24.

5. Psalm 68:5.

6. Isaiah 55:9.

7. Barbara Bush, *A Memoir* (New York: Scribner, 1994), 248–49.

Chapter Eleven: Dying *for*, Not *with,* Your Dreams

1. John 10:10.

2. Oswald Chambers, *My Utmost for His Highest* (New York: Dodd, Mead, 1935), 71.

3. Buck Tilton, "Paul Petzoldt's 'Grand' Finale," *Backpacker* (December 1994), 14.

4. James 1:5–6.

5. Isaiah 43:2–3.

6. Charles R. Swindoll, *Laugh Again* (Waco: Word, 1992), 69–70.

7. Ibid., 156–60.